LITTLE BOOK OF

Musicals

LITTLE BOOK OF

Musicals

First published in the UK in 2014

© Demand Media Limited 2014

www.demand-media.co.uk

Printed and bound in Europe

ISBN 978-1-910270-10-3

Contents

Foreword

During the last hundred years or so the musical theatre has offered numerous descriptive sub-titles for its staged products. The Gilbert and Sullivan works and their rivals saw themselves quite logically as comic operas, following Offenbach's chosen 'opera comique'. The next generation of musical shows tended to prefer the title of 'musical comedy'. Because the popular theatres had no place for 'musical tragedies' the word comedy became pointless and the single title of 'musical' came into common use. And so it has remained. A musical is quite simply a romantic story enlivened by music of a popular nature - in many shapes and forms. The work that many would choose as the best musical of all - 'My Fair Lady' - is successful because its libretto is George Bernard Shaw's superb comedy 'Pygmalion' more or less intact enhanced by a musical score of unrivalled aptness and grace. All of the fifty musicals discussed in this book are perfect in their own way - 'Oklahoma', 'Oliver', 'Show Boat' - with 'Porgy and Bess' a work of such musical substance that it is very often categorised as an 'opera'. Somebody else's choice of fifty titles would not be very different. And anyone who can claim to have heard and knows all of these works could be one the luckiest people around. The world of the musical is a world of sheer enjoyment, a world of laughter and tears perfectly blended with a sauce of greatly unforgettable tunes. This is the world of the Musical tastefully dissected!

Peter Gammond

Author of the Oxford Companion to Popular Music

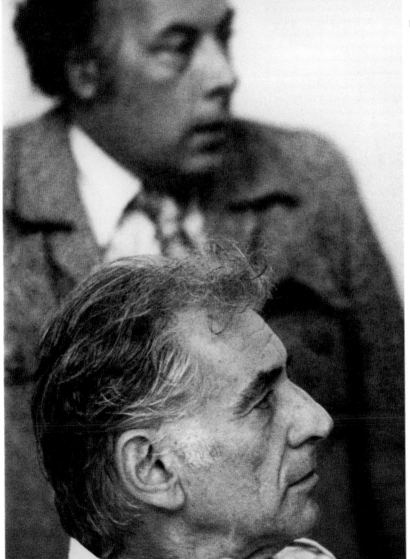

Left: *Peter Gammond with composer Leonard Bernstein in Paris 1988.*

Introduction

What is the musical? It is difficult to identify with great clarity exactly what the musical is, however it would be true to say that it is very much a living art form.

Musicals are constantly evolving and have been doing so for the last few centuries, both on stage and screen. Most musicals can be identified in that they tell a story, with either song, or song and optional dialogue, enabling them to showcase the talents of the performers and writers.

Historically, musicals were termed as comic operas, operettas, burlesques, extravaganzas and musical comedies. However, they also had their roots in variety, vaudeville, musicals and minstrel shows.

Musicals that stand the test of time must have many essential qualities including great songs and music, interesting characters, believability and be both creative and entertaining.

As to how long ago they were first performed, you can go back to both Greek and Roman times. Playwrights from both eras were known to have included music and dance in performances often being staged in open air amphitheatres, often featuring sexual humour, and political and social satire – the purpose being to entertain the masses by any means possible.

During the Middle Ages, Europe was home to many travelling minstrels and troops of players that performed both popular songs and slapstick comedy.

The question has long been asked, are musicals descended from opera? Although operas have evolved since the late 1500s, it is not thought that contemporary

musical theatre and film are descendants of either classic theatre or opera. Many early musicals often spoofed opera but it is easier to trace the lineage of musicals from the vaudevilles and burlesques of the day.

Musicals have been with us for hundreds of years. Although the aspect of musicals overlaps with other theatrical forms such as opera and dance, the musical theatre can be seen as a combination of songs, acting, spoken dialogue and dance.

The communication of humour, love and anger are told through words, music and movement.

One of the forerunners to our modern day musical was written by John Gay in 1728, and was called *The Beggars Opera* running for 62 performances at the Lincolns Inn Fields. This broke records at the time and manager of the theatre, John Rich, who had initially been reluctant to stage the play made so much money from

Above: *A scene from The Beggar's Opera 1729*

the production that he built a new theatre in Covent Garden which stood in place of the Royal Opera House.

The Beggars Opera became popular due to clever use of familiar tunes and using characters that its audience could identify with. The music for the show included popular songs of the time with the story being a satire on an Italian dramatic opera which had been popular in London at that time.

During the Victorian era, burlesques became a popular way of entertaining the masses. These featured exaggerated costumes with on occasion, leading actresses showing their legs in britches which were scandalous for this age. Burlesque usually satirized well known plays, stories and operas, many of the burlesques were full of puns and wordplays which were popular at the time.

During this era, two famous writers, Gilbert and Sullivan came to the fore. The pair wrote 14 operettas together between 1871 and 1896 but were involved in many other productions. It was thanks to London theatre manager Richard D'Oyly Carte that the two came together; after asking successful playwright Gilbert to produce a new piece for him, he recommended Sullivan and the pair produced *Trial By Jury*, which became a huge success.

Riding high on the success of this

production D'Oyly Carte took a huge risk and leased another London theatre and founded the Comedy Opera Company. Both Gilbert and Sullivan had agreed to write him a full length opera, the first, called *The Sorcerer,* opened in 1877 and was then followed by *HMS Pinafore.*

Unauthorised versions of several of Gilbert and Sullivan's operettas had been staged in America and upon hearing this, Gilbert was so furious that he used the issue of piracy to inspire his next libretto, *The Pirates of Penzance.* In an attempt to resolve this problem, D'Oyly Carte ensured that the production opened on the same day in December 1879 both in New York and London.

Gilbert and Sullivan operas became so popular in the late 1800s, that a new theatre was built especially to house them. The Savoy Opera opened in April 1881 and for over the next 15 years people flocked to see the pair's hugely successful operas.

It is interesting to note that it was mainly due to the charm and persuasiveness of D'Oyly Carte which kept the partnership between Gilbert and Sullivan in tact. They were reportedly constantly at loggerheads with each other.

Although hugely successful with his comic operas, Sullivan was still ambitious to garner the same success in writing grand opera. Yet again, D'Oyly Carte stepped in to help him realise this goal by building the Royal English Opera house. Sullivan's first grand opera, *Ivanhoe* opened at the Royal English Opera house in January 1891 and although popular, the public were never to show the same appreciation and enthusiasm as they did for the cheerful and witty works created by both Gilbert and Sullivan.

Even in modern day musical theatre, Gilbert and Sullivan's influence is profound: they found ways to integrate musicals so that both the lyrics and dialogue are designed to create a coherent story. Many famous authors and composers of musicals have long admired their works, including PG Woodhouse, Jerome Kern, Ira Gershwin, Irving Berlin, Ivor Novello, Oscar Hammerstein and Andrew Lloyd Webber.

During the 1870s and 80s, musicals began to attract much more attention from respectable audiences in a marked contrast from the bawdy musical shows and risqué burlesques of the past.

On Broadway, many hundreds of musical comedies were being staged in the early 20th century, however their runs continued to be relatively short compared to London runs until the 1920s. However, taking their musicals on tour became commonplace in America.

After leaving the Savoy Theatre, George Edwardes took over the Gaiety Theatre and started to produce a more family friendly musical theatre style, using breezy popular songs and snappy romantic banter. These became hugely successful, with the bawdy women of the burlesque being replaced with respectable corps of dancing girls. Both *In Town*, produced in 1892 and *The Gaiety Girl* in 1893 revolutionised the London stage and was to set the tone in musical production and direction for the next three decades.

Having been virtually eliminated by the Edwardian musical comedies in 1890s, operetta made a return to both London and Broadway in 1907 with the production of *The Merry Widow*; several others were to follow however during World War One. Not surprisingly, the German language operetta lost its popularity.

The need for escapist entertainment during WWI saw the hit musical *Irene* running for a record-breaking 670 performances on Broadway. Likewise, in Britain, *Maid of the Mountains* ran for 1352 performances and *Chu Chin Chow* ran for 2238 performances, more than twice as many as previous musicals. This set the record for nearly 40 years, not to be broken until the long running production of *Salad Days*.

By 1920, the gradual American evolution in musicals spearheaded by the likes of Charles Frohman and Jerome Kern began to replace the dominance of British musical theatre. Both ragtime and jazz styled musicals began to take hold with the Shubert brothers and other new writers such as George and Ira Gershwin, Rodgers and Hart producing many popular musicals of that era.

During the Roaring Twenties, musicals tended to include big dance routines, popular songs and more emphasis on star actors and actresses, sadly sometimes at the expense of the plot.

Famous stars such as Fred Astaire and Marilyn Miller became popular during this era in America; meanwhile stars such as Ivor Novello and Noel Coward were becoming equally famous in London. The production of *Showboat* in 1927 at the Ziegfeld Theatre created a completely new genre, distinguishing the musical play from the musical comedy.

The Great Depression of the 1930s

affected audiences on both sides of the Atlantic with only a few stage shows exceeding their runs on either Broadway or London.

The 1940s saw the completion of the revolution in musical history created by *Showboat* with the opening of Rogers and Hammerstein's *Oklahoma!* It became the first blockbuster Broadway show, running for more than 2000 performances, defying musical conventions by raising the curtain not to a bevy of chorus girls but rather a bunch of rather plain women churning their butter with the song *"Oh What a Beautiful Mornin' "* being sung off stage. Rodgers and Hammerstein became some of the most important contributors to the musical play form, going on to produce some of musical theatre's best loved and most enduring classics which include *Carousel*, *South Pacific*, *The King and I* and *The Sound of Music*.

Now the golden age of American musical theatre arrived, the formula for these reflecting the widely held perceptions of the American dream. Namely that stability and worth derives from a loving relationship which has been sanctioned by the ideals of marriage, that married couples should make a moral home for their children away from cities and that the woman's place was in the home and the idea that Americans incorporate a pioneering spirit or being self made successes.

Above: *Jose Collins as Teresa in The Maid of The Mountains*

Right: *My Fair Lady – one of the best musicals of the century*

The 1950s was to see the beginning of many long-running shows such as *My Fair Lady*, starring Rex Harrison and Julie Andrews and *The Boyfriend*, which ran for more than 2000 performances in London, becoming the third longest running musical in the West End and Broadway's history.

Towards the end of the 50s, *West Side Story*, created by Leonard Bernstein and Stephen Sondheim premiered, but although being popular with the critics, it failed to wow its audiences. When Sondheim and Arthur Lawrence teamed up again to produce *Gypsy*, the show enjoyed renewed success, running for 700 performances and being revived four times.

The Sound of Music was the last hit created by Rodgers and Hammerstein, it opened at the end of the 50's and ran for many years becoming one of the most popular musicals in history.

The 1970s were to see the flourishing of the new genre of rock musicals. Many of these rock musicals began with concept albums, then moving onto film and stage. These included such productions as *Tommy*, *Jesus Christ Superstar*, *Godspell*, *The Rocky Horror Show* and *Two Gentlemen of Verona*.

When *A Chorus Line* was bought to the stage in 1975, it was a huge success, becoming the longest running production in Broadway history up to that time running for more than 6000 performances and sweeping the board at the Tony awards that year.

Towards the end of the decade, productions such as *Evita* and *Sweeney Todd* were to become the precursors too much darker, big budget musicals to be produced in the 1980s, which depended on more dramatic stories, sweeping scores and spectacular visual effects.

The 1980s were to see European style "mega musicals" arrive onto the stages of Broadway, the West End and elsewhere in the world. Most of these works were to feature pop influenced scores, big budget shows with large casts and sets and being identified for notable effects such as the falling chandelier in the *Phantom of the Opera* and a helicopter landing on the stage in *Miss Saigon*.

Andrew Lloyd Webber was to become world famous, producing musicals such as *Evita*, *Cats*, *Starlight Express* and the *Phantom of the Opera*. These shows had extraordinary international success and were the beginning of mega-musicals that relied on huge budgets. With the multi-million dollar production costs, these shows needed to run for years simply to turn a profit.

Despite the growing number of large-scale musicals in both the 80s and 90s such as Walt Disney's *Beauty and the Beast* and the *Lion King*, a number of low budget, smaller scale musicals had managed to find both critical and financial success. These included such productions as the *Little Shop of Horrors* and *Blood Brothers*.

In more recent times, both producers and investors have used familiar themes to guarantee the return on their investments and in turn hopefully show a healthy profit. However, some new and unusual productions such as *Urinetown* have taken a chance and been successful on the stage. Many revivals have been given the kiss of life, as they have proven material with hopefully a built in audience to create profit: these include the likes of *South Pacific*, *Gypsy*, *West Side Story* and *Fiddler on the Roof*.

The emergence of jukebox musicals where a minimal plot is created to fit a collection of songs has recently being very successful, including the likes of *Mama Mia!*, *Buddy - the Buddy Holly Story* and *Jersey Boys*.

The history of musicals has been evolving and changing for many generations, and it is clear that the musical is still a living and growing genre. It is unlikely to see a return to the so-called golden age of musicals as public taste has undergone fundamental changes, however spectacular musicals have been and always will be popular tourist attractions and, at the end of the day, still offer a great night out!

A Chorus Line

Having opened on Broadway in 1975 at the Shubert Theatre, A Chorus Line was the longest running Broadway musical to be originally produced in the US until the advent of Cats. It still remains the sixth longest running Broadway show of all time, with 6137 performances and went on a worldwide tour including a lengthy spell in the West End in 1976.

The Public Theatre, off Broadway, had to borrow $1.6 million to produce the show. However there was a huge demand to see the musical and the entire run sold out immediately. In 1976, it received 12 Tony award nominations and won nine of them; it also won the 1976 Pulitzer Prize for Drama, a rare and well deserved accolade for a musical.

In London, A Chorus Line opened at the Royal Drury Lane Theatre in 1976. It won the Laurence Olivier award for Best Musical, a special honour, as it was the inaugural year of the ceremony.

The story behind A Chorus Line originated from workshop sessions held by Michael Bennett and his fellow chorus line dancers working on Broadway. These dancers, commonly termed gypsies on Broadway, were paid a hundred dollars a week to talk about their personal and professional lives. Michael had the idea of using these insights and experiences to produce a musical libretto. James Kirkwood Jr and Nicolas Dante turned the resulting work into a book. The music was written by Marvin Hamlisch with lyrics written by Edward Kleban

The resulting musical was highly unusual, and called an "anti-musical" in

the States, as it had no real costumes and very little scenery apart from mirrors. It also had no main star or intermission.

A Chorus Line has been revived both on Broadway in 2006 and in the West End in 2013.

Annie

Opposite: *Annie programme*

Annie opened on Broadway in 1977 setting a record for the Alvin Theatre, now renamed the Neil Simon Theatre, where it ran for nearly six years.

The musical was based upon a comic strip called Little Orphan Annie by Harold Gray. Thomas Meehan wrote the spin-off book and received the Tony award for Best Book of a Musical three times. The music was composed by Charles Strousse and the original lyrics were written by Martin Charnin.

The story of Annie is set in the 1930s. Annie is a young orphan living in an orphanage run by the corrupt Miss Hannigan. She decides to run away and find her parents but is eventually caught and returned to the orphanage. As luck would have it, she goes to stay with a billionaire for the Christmas holidays who eventually warms to Annie. He decides to help her find her parents by offering a large reward. The corrupt Miss Hannigan aided by her brother and girlfriend try to defraud the billionaire by pretending to be Annie's long lost parents. However all ends well!

The show contains several very popular songs including "Tomorrow" and "Hard Knock Life" – the latter being adapted for use by the character Dr Evil in the Austen Powers film Goldmember.

In 1976, Annie had its first pre-Broadway trial at the Goodspeed Opera House in Connecticut. After the first week, it was decided that the star Kristen Vigard was too sweet natured in the role of Annie and she was replaced by Andrea McArdle who had been playing the part of one of the other orphans in the performance.

Annie was nominated for 11 Tony Awards in 1977, winning seven including

Best Musical, Best Score and Best Book.

In 1978, the musical opened in the West End, playing at the Victoria Palace Theatre. Andrea McArdle was brought over from America to play the role of Annie, and starred in 40 performances. After this, the role was taken over by Anne Marie Gwatkin, who appeared on the original London cast recording, though the role was subsequently cast to myriad other Annies from then on.

Touring Annie in Britain was to become more complicated than in America. The rather stringent British employment laws with regards to juvenile actors necessitated that every four months the star of the show should be changed.

In 1977 Annie was subject to a revival on Broadway. This performance was surrounded in controversy. The original actress had been fired whilst suffering from bronchitis. Claims of racism were also bandied about as commercials promoting the show used a white actress instead of the black actress Nell Carter who was to play the part of Miss Hannigan, the Orphanage Manager.

Annie went on to be made into several films, in 1982, 1999 and 2014, the most recent starring actor Will Smith's daughter Willow.

Billy Elliot

Opposite: Poster
of the film version

Billy Elliot was originally an award-winning film before it was converted into a stage musical in 2005 with similar stunning success.

Both the musical and film originate from a book written by Lee Hall, who wrote the screenplay for the film and also the lyrics for the musical.

Set during the mid-1980s miners' strike, 11 year-old Billie loves to dance and has aspirations of becoming a professional ballet dancer. However his father and elder brother are both coal miners and are out on strike.

Billy's father tries to make him learn boxing, which he hates, but he happens upon a ballet class in the same gym. He secretly joins the ballet class and when his father discovers this, he is mortified.

Billy's ballet teacher believes he should audition for a place at the Royal Ballet School in London. However he misses the audition due to his brother's arrest during a skirmish with the striking miners and police.

Finally Billy's father recognises his son's talent when secretly watching him dance and although risking breaking the strike, the local pit communities agree to help finance Billy to go to London and audition.

Billy Elliot is a heartwarming story of a young boy who manages to reach beyond the constraints of his world and to successfully fight for his dream of becoming a ballet dancer.

Music for Billy Elliot was written by Elton John who having seen the film at the Cannes Film Festival, was reduced to tears and became convinced that the story could work well as a musical.

The original musical was to have

premiered in Newcastle upon Tyne at the Tyne but a financial fog meant it never saw the light of day. Finally in March 2005 Billy Elliot premiered in the West End at the Victoria Palace Theatre, officially opening on 11th May 2005. It was nominated for nine Laurence Olivier Awards and went on to win four, including Best New Musical. It is still wowing audiences to this day and is planned to run until at least 2015.

The original London production was directed by Stephen Daltrey, the choreographer being Peter Darling, who had both also worked on the original film.

In New York, Billy Elliot was as successful as it was in the UK, winning 10 Tony Awards and Drama Desk Awards apiece.

Unusually, the orchestra for Billy Elliot is so large that it requires many extra instruments. On Broadway, there were 17 musicians, with nearly all the players having to double on two or more instruments.

Buddy

Right: *Cover of the CD of the Cast Recording*

Buddy is the musical based on the life and career of rock'n'roll star Buddy Holly.

The show was the idea of Laurie Mansfield who, after talking with film producer Greg Smith and writer Alan James, finally secured support for the project from Paul McCartney. Paul Elliot was brought in to produce the musical which premiered in London in 1989.

The musical follows the story of Buddy and his two friends Joe and Jerry who form a band called The Crickets. As they begin to cast their career in the music world, they meet and sign a contract with Norman Petty, a new and up-and-coming record producer. Almost straight after their first meeting, one of Buddy's biggest hit songs "That'll Be the Day" was recorded and within a matter of weeks, Buddy Holly and The Crickets became one of the most successful bands in the country.

In New York, Buddy meets and falls in love with Maria, they have a whirlwind romance and marry after a courtship of only five hours. Sadly, the band squabble and Buddy decides to pursue a solo career. Although promising his now pregnant wife not to fly during his last ill-fated tour, after his final performance in Iowa with Ritchie

and humour.

The musical opened at the Victoria Palace Theatre on London's West End and remained there for six years, it was then transferred to the Strand Theatre and has run for another six and a half years with a total of over five thousand performances, making it one of London's longest running musicals.

Buddy was also produced on Broadway in 1990, opening at the Shubert Theatre and running for 225 performances.

The show has been successful whilst on tour. In 2000 the show toured for a 27 city run in America and is due to commence a 25th anniversary tour in the UK.

In 1991, Buddy Holly was nominated for Best New Musical and Paul Hipp, portraying the role of Buddy was nominated for Outstanding Performance of the Year by an Actor in a Musical at the Laurence Olivier Awards. Whilst the show played on Broadway, Paul Hipp was again nominated for Best Actor in a Musical at the Tony Awards, Outstanding Actor in a Musical at the Drama Desk Awards and won the coveted World Theatre Award.

The show is a true rock'n'roll extravaganza and features some of Buddy Holly's most famous hits including "That'll be the Day", "Peggy Sue", "Oh Boy" and "Heartbeat."

Valens and the big bopper JP Richardson, the three board a small plane in Iowa and take off for Minnesota. Tragically, the plane crashes into a ploughed field after takeoff leaving no survivors. The life of Buddy Holly has become the stuff of legend, with the musical being a celebration of the life and times of a man that caught the attention of many for his mixture of innocence, talent, determination

Bugsy Malone

Bugsy Malone was a highly-original spoof gangster drama with children taking the lead roles as mobsters and molls. It was first seen in the West End at Her Majesty's Theatre on 23rd May 1983 where it ran for 300 performances.

Unanimously praised by the critics, the music was created by Oscar-nominated composer and lyricist Paul Williams. Although the cast featured children, adults were providing the vocals off stage.

The National Youth Music Theatre went on to produce an all-child cast of Bugsy Malone in 1997 opening at the Queens Theatre on 21st November. Sheridan Smith led the 40-strong ensemble while the role of Tallulah was played by a young Catherine Zeta-Jones in the West End production.

The original story of Bugsy Malone was created from a book by Alan Parker who went on to direct the feature film starring child actress Jodie Foster and Scott Baio.

Set in 1929 Chicago, the story features characters such as mob boss Fat Sam, his arch rival Dandy Dan, aspiring singer Blousy Brown, femme fatale Tallulah and boxing contendor Leroy.

The finale at Fat Sam's club features a massive splurge gunfight with foam custard pies taking the place of bullets. It was all great harmless humourous fun punctuated with brilliantly catchy tunes such as 'You Give A Little Love" and "So You Want To Be A Boxer".

In 2003, Channel 4 viewers voted Bugsy Malone number 19 on a list of the 100 greatest musicals, placing it higher than The Phantom of the Opera, The King and I, and Cats!

EVERY YEAR BRINGS A GREAT MOVIE.
EVERY DECADE A GREAT MOVIE MUSICAL!

PARAMOUNT PICTURES PRESENTS A ROBERT STIGWOOD PRESENTATION
A GOODTIMES ENTERPRISES PRODUCTION OF
ALAN PARKER'S FILM

"BUGSY MALONE"

JODIE FOSTER as Tallulah   SCOTT BAIO as Bugsy   FLORRIE DUGGER as Blousey   JOHN CASSISI as Fat Sam

Cabaret

Opposite:
*Cabaret
programme*

The stage version of Cabaret - best known as a Oscar-winning film starring Liza Minelli and Michael York - was first seen on Broadway in 1966 and has since been repeatedly revived around the world earning 'money, money, money' for its producers.

Based upon the book Goodbye To Berlin, written by Christopher Isherwood in 1939 - which went on to become a play called I Am A Camera, written by John Van Druten in 1951 – the Broadway show was produced by Hal Prince, with music by John Kander and lyrics by Fred Ebb.

The musical ran for more than 1000 performances and had similar success in the West End where it opened at the Palace Theatre in 1968, and ran for 336 performances starring Judi Dench, Barry Dennen and Peter Sallis.

Set in 1931 Berlin, as the Nazis are rising to power, it is based in the seedy Kit Kat Klub and revolves around scatty 19-year-old English cabaret performer Sally Bowles and her relationship with the young American writer Cliff Bradshaw.

A sub-plot involves the doomed romance between a ravishing German girl Fräulein Schneider and her elderly suitor Herr Schultz, a Jewish fruit vendor. Overseeing the action is the charismatic Master of Ceremonies at the Kit Kat Klub with the goings-on at the club serving as a metaphor for the threatening state of late Weimar Germany.

The show has had many popular revivals, initially at the Strand Theatre in 1986 starring Kelly Hunter, Peter Land and Wayne Sleep, and at the Imperial Theatre on Broadway in 1987 where it was again directed by Harold Prince with the choreography by Ron Field.

In 1993, a darker Cabaret was revived at the Donmar Warehouse, directed by the Sam Mendes and starring Jane Horrocks, Adam Godley, Alan Cumming and Sara Kestelman, who won an Olivier award for Best Supporting Performance in a Musical.

Again on Broadway, Cabaret was revived for the second time in 1998 and was nominated for 10 Tony awards, winning four including Best Revival of a Musical. It finished at Studio 54 becoming the third longest running revival on Broadway with 2377 performances.

There have been other revivals, most notably in London both in 2006 and 2012. The most recent playing at the Savoy Theatre in the West End following a four week tour of the UK, starring Will Young, Michelle Ryan, Sian Phillips and Matt Rawle.

In 2014 Cabaret returns to Studio 54 in New York. Both Sam Mendes and Robert Marshall will be working on the show as director and choreographer, with Alan Cumming returning to star alongside Michelle Williams who will be making her Broadway debut.

Harold Prince & Richard Pilbrow
(in association with Ruth Mitchell)
present

CABARET
AT THE PALACE THEATRE

PROGRAMME
ONE SHILLING

LICENSED BY THE LORD CHAMBERLAIN TO AND
UNDER THE MANAGEMENT OF EMILE LITTLER

Carousel

Carousel was an immediate hit with both critics and audiences when opening on Broadway in April 1945.

It was the second musical produced by Rodgers and Hammerstein which followed hot on the heels of their spectacular first hit musical Oklahoma! which they produced in 1943.

Carousel was adapted from Liliom, a play written in 1909 by the Ferenc Molnar. The play was premiered in Budapest, initially in Hungarian, and was not a success, only lasting for 30 performances before being withdrawn. However, when it eventually reappeared on the stage in Budapest after the First World War, it became a tremendous hit.

The story revolves around carousel barker Billy Bigelow, whose romance with millworker Julie Jordan comes at the price of both their jobs. He attempts a robbery to provide for Julie and their unborn child; after it goes fatally wrong, he is given a chance to make things right.

A secondary plot line deals with millworker Carrie Pipperidge and her romance with ambitious fisherman Enoch Snow. The show includes the well-known songs "If I Loved You", "June is Bustin Out All Over" and " You'll Never Walk Alone" (which is to this day sung by supporters of Liverpool Football Club as their team's anthem). Richard Rodgers later proclaimed that Carousel was his favorite of all his musicals.

The idea to turn the play into a musical was suggested to Rodgers and Hammerstein by Theresa Helburn and Lawrence Langner of the Theatre Guild over lunch. However, both men refused, as they believed the unhappy ending would be unsuitable for musical theatre. However, when Rodgers

suggested that they change the setting of the play from Budapest to New England, Hammerstein finally agreed.

The musical opened at the Majestic Theatre on Broadway in 1945. The dress rehearsal had gone so badly that both Rodgers Hammerstein believed the musical would be a flop. Their fears were unfounded and the show was met with wild applause and rave reviews from the critics. It went on to run for 890 performances, closing in 1947. After this, the musical toured for two years in America with a five-month stint in Chicago. The production in 1945 was awarded eight Donaldson Awards (these pre-dated the Tony awards) and also won the new York Drama Critics Circle Award for Best Musical.

In 1950, Carousel went on to premiere at the Theatre Royal, Drury Lane in London's West End. It ran for 566 performances, playing for more than a year and a half. The show has enjoyed many revivals and was made into a film in 1956 starring Gordon MacRae and Shirley Jones.

The 1992 London revival saw the musical winning numerous Olivier Awards including Best Musical Revival and Best Director. When this production moved to Broadway, it also won five Tony Awards, three Drama Desk Awards and two Theatre World Awards.

Cats

Opposite: *The famous CATS logo*

Cats is the second highest grossing musical of all time, after The Phantom Of The Opera. It has been seen by more than 50 million people in 300 cities across the globe including Buenos Aires, Seoul, Helsinki and Singapore.

The music for Cats was written by Andrew Lloyd Webber. It was based on Old Possum's Book of Practical Cats by T.S. Eliot. The show was produced by Cameron Mackintosh.

The musical tells the story of a tribe of cats called the Jellicles. It describes the night when they make what is known as "the Jellicle choice" and decide which cat will ascend to the Heaviside Layer and come back to a new life.

It won many awards, including Best Musical at both the Laurence Olivier Awards and the Tony Awards. The London production ran for 21 years and the Broadway production ran for 18 years, both setting new records. Lead performers Elaine Paige and Betty Buckley became particularly associated with the show while actress Marlene Danielle played in the Broadway production for its entire run (from 1982 until 2000).

Cats is the second longest-running show in Broadway history, and is the fourth longest-running West End musical. It has been performed around the world wide many times and has been translated into more than 20 languages. In 1998, Cats was made into a film for television.

T.S. Eliot's Old Possum's Book of Practical Cats (1939) was one of composer Andrew Lloyd Weber's favourite childhood books. Nearly

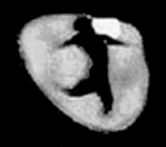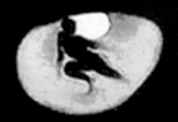

CATS

all the songs of the musical are made up of Eliot's verse set to music by the composer. The exception was actually the most famous song from the musical - "Memory" - the lyrics for which were written by Trevor Nunn based on the T.S. Eliot poem called "Rhapsody on a Windy Night".

In 1977, Andrew Lloyd Webber began composing the songs for Cats and premiered the compositions at the Sydmonton Festival in 1980. The wife of T.S. Eliot, attended the festival, loved the songs and gave her blessing for them to be adapted into a musical stage play.

In early 1981, rehearsals for the musical began at the New London Theatre. The Eliot estate had asked that no script was to be written and that the original poems were to be used as the text. Subsequently, the musical had no identifiable plot and many of the actors were confused about what they were actually doing in rehearsals.

The overture of Cats was extremely unusual as it incorporated a fugue while there is very little spoken dialogue in the show, as it is told nearly all through music.

Set in a large junk yard, the dancing in Cats plays an integral part of the show especially in the Jellicle Ball dance sequence. The original first night in the West End at the New London Theatre had to be postponed when actress Judi Dench suffered a torn achilles tendon and Elaine Paige took over the part of Grizabella.

It finally opened on 11th of May 1981 with a cast that included Elaine Paige, Brian Blessed, Paul Nicholas, Wayne Sleep, Sarah Brightman and Bonnie Langford. Elaine Paige went on to have a hit single with the song Memory from the show and the cast won a Grammy Award. The original production also won two Laurence Olivier Awards in 1981.

Since then, it has taken £136m at London box offices and a further £1.25bn worldwide.

After 8,949 performances in London's West End, the curtain finally came down on its 21st birthday, 11th of May 2002. It was also broadcasted on a large screen in Covent Garden to the delight of fans who could not acquire a ticket for the final performance. It held the record as London's longest running musical until 8th of October 2006, when it was surpassed by Les Misérables.

Charlie and the Chocolate Factory

Roald Dahl's deliciously dark tale of young Charlie Bucket and the mysterious confectioner Willy Wonka has been brought to life in a brand new West End musical directed by Academy Award winner Sam Mendes.

Written by David Greig, with the music and lyrics by Marc Shaiman and Scott Wittman, Mendes was working on the Bond movie Sky Fall whilst directing Charlie and the Chocolate Factory.

He had invited Grieg to write the musical in 2009 but the Scottish playwright, who had not been heavily involved in the musicals before, initially believed that it was going to be impossible to produce. However, he was convinced by Mendes that as long as he wrote the story, the team would work out how to stage it.

The original story of Charlie and the Chocolate Factory was written by Dahl and tells the macabre tale of a young boy called Charlie Bucket, his poor family and the mysterious reclusive confectioner Willy Wonka.

Wonka has not been seen in years as he closed his chocolate factory to public access after his competitors, most specifically Arthur Slugworth, infiltrated the factory to steal his candy secrets. However, Wonka allows access to his factory but only to five people and a guest apiece, each of whom will be given a lifetime's supply of chocolate. Those five will be those that find one of the five golden tickets hidden inside Wonka chocolate bars.

Although Charlie's chances of getting a golden ticket are remote at best – especially against a glutton, a spoiled peanut heiress, a gum fanatic and a television fanatic – Charlie wants it more than anyone else and it is the small dream which is keeping his spirit alive. Those that eventually get the golden tickets will be exposed to all of Wonka's magical secrets, the latest rumored to be that of the everlasting gobstopper, a sweet that never gets smaller. But they will also be treated to an experience that some will hopefully learn from. And one will learn the real reason for Wonka providing access to the factory.

Charlie and the Chocolate Factory premiered at the Theatre Royal, Drury Lane in London's West End in June 2013. The design of the huge number of amazing scenes during the show were created by Mark Thompson, who went on to win the 2014 What's On Stage.com Awards for Best Set Designer; with Peter Darling winning Best Choreographer.

The production – which stars Douglas Hodge (as Willy Wonka) and Nigel Planer best known as the hippy Neil from The Young Ones – was also nominated by the Evening Standard Awards for Best Night Out in 2013.

Although the show has only been on stage briefly, the production has already extended the performances until May 2015, and only six months after its

premiere, the show has set a new West End Theatre record.

Charlie and the Chocolate Factory is also a 2005 film directed by Tim Burton. It is the second film adaptation of Dahl's 1964 book and stars Johnny Depp as Willy Wonka and Freddie Highmore as Charlie Bucket.

Above: Cover of the CD

Chigaco

Opposite: *Poster for the musical*

Chicago first opened on Broadway in 1975 at the 46th Street Theatre. It ran for 936 performances and closed in 1977. The original choreographer was Bob Fosse. The show then moved to London's West End in 1979 and ran for 600 performances. Chicago was revived in both Broadway and the West End in the 1990s, and went on to be the longest running revival on Broadway, playing over 6,700 performances. In the West End, the show ran for nearly 15 years, the revival became the longest running American musical.

The musical Chicago was based on a 1926 play by reporter Maurine Dallas Watkins. The music was composed by John Kander, with the lyrics by Fred Ebb. There is a book of the same name written by Ebb and Bob Fosse.

Watkins, reporting at the time for the Chicago Tribune, was covering the trials in 1924 of Beulah Annan and Belva Gaertner, both of whom were on trial for murder. The cases sparked off a media war between the Hearst Papers, who were more pro-defendant, and the Chicago Tribune who were more pro-prosecution. Both papers made out that the defendants were celebrities of the day rather than defendants in murder trials. From the popularity of her column during these trials, Watkins wrote the play of Chicago which went on to run on Broadway. There have been several films made from the original play: Cecil B. deMille produced a silent film in 1927 and Ginger Rogers starred in the remake in 1942.

Another remake of Chicago in 2002, won six Academy awards, starred Renée Zellweger, Catherine Zeta-

Jones, Richard Gere, John C. Reilly, and Queen Latifah and was directed by Rob Marshall.

The idea to create a musical was first initiated in the 1960s. Bob Fosse approached Watkins to buy the rights to the play. However, by this time, Watkins had become a born-again Christian, and believed that her play had glamorised a sinful and scandalous way of living and refused. It was only after her death that the rights of the play were sold.

The musical score was produced by John Kander and Fred Ebb. They successfully modelled each song on either a vaudeville number or performer to show the difference between the reality and the show business effect caused by the newspapers handling of the cases.

When it opened in 1975, Chicago was not an initial success. Indeed, the cynical style of the show was said to make the audiences uncomfortable. It also opened in the same year as the very successful A Chorus Line.

The show nearly had to close after Gwen Verdon, playing the role of Roxie Hart, needed an operation after breathing in a feather in the finale. However, Liza Minelli was found as her replacement and stayed with the show for a month whilst Verdon recuperated. Not surprisingly, during this time, the shows popularity increased.

Chicago opened in the West End in 1979 at the Cambridge Theatre, and ran for 600 performances, starring Jenny Logan, Ben Cross and Antonia Ellis as Roxie. The show was nominated as Musical of the Year, while both Cross and Ellis were nominated for an Laurence Olivier Award following their performances.

The revival of Chicago in 1996 became the fastest show to recover its initial costs, partly due to the minimalist set and partly as the American audience were more receptive to the cynical viewpoint taken from the play. The show had a new script written by David Thompson and directed by Walter Bobbie. The original star of the show, Ann Reinking who played Roxie Hart was very instrumental in this revival.

The popularity of the show was enhanced by winning no less than six Tony awards in 1997 including Best Revival, two Olivier awards and a Grammy.

Back in the UK, the revival of Chicago was put on stage originally at the Adelphi Theatre in 1997, before moving to the Cambridge Theatre in 2006, then

finally transferring to the Garrick theatre in 2011. It was equally successful as its American counterpart, winning the 1998 Olivier Award for Outstanding Musical and running for 15 years.

Many celebrities starred in the British revival including Marti Pellow, David Hasselhoff, John Barrowman, Maria Friedman, Josefina Gabrielle, Denise Van Outen, Claire Sweeney, Linzi Hateley, Frances Ruffelle, Jennifer Ellison, Jill Halfpenny, Brooke Shields, Sally Ann Triplett, Bonnie Langford, Tina Arena, Ashlee Simpson, Aoife Mulholland, Michelle Williams and Christie Brinkley.

Above: *Poster for the musical*

Chitty Chitty Bang Bang

The musical of Chitty Chitty Bang Bang was based upon the blockbuster movie, produced by Albert R Broccoli in 1968, and inspired by the children's book written by Ian Fleming, author of the James Bond spy novels.

The title is taken from the name of an extraordinary flying car whose eccentric inventor, Caractacus Potts is embroiled in a plot to outwit the dastardly Baron and evil Child Catcher. – helped by various family members and quirky friends.

In 2002, the musical premiered at the London Palladium in the West End. Six new songs were written for the show by the Sherman Brothers (who had written the original film score which had been nominated for an Academy Award) while it was directed by Adrian Noble.

Gillian Lynne was the choreographer and also staged the music.

Chitty Chitty Bang Bang was a huge success, taking over £70 million in just three and a half years and becoming the longest running show at the London Palladium. Actors starring in the original show included Michael Ball, Emma Williams and Brian Blessed. Many other respected British actors have also starred in the London production including Brian Conley, Gary Wilmot, Christopher Biggins, Paul O'Grady, Lionel Blair, Wayne Sleep and Russ Abbot.

The show opened in the Foxwoods Theatre, Broadway in April 2005. Both Noble and Lynne had come to oversee direction and choreography. However the reviews were not good and the production was to close after only 285

performances in December of the same year.

The musical has continued to play to full houses across the UK and has also been produced at the Capital Theatre in Sydney, Australia in November 2012.

Evita

Evita premiered in London's West End in 1978 and has bought nothing but tears of joy for its creator Tim Rice.

Its unlikely and tragic storyline concerns Eva Peron, an iconic political leader of Argentina and wife of the president.

The idea for the musical came from Tim Rice who had always been intrigued by the character of Eva Peron. Indeed, he had travelled to Buenos Aires to carry out research and had also named his daughter after her.

However when he had suggested the idea to his writing partner Andrew Lloyd Webber, it was initially rejected. Lloyd Webber went on to produce a musical with playwright Alan Ayckbourn called Jeeves. After this turned out to be a flop, Lloyd Webber and Rice began developing the musical of Evita.

The musical was first performed at the second Sydmonton Festival, conducted by Anthony Bowles, and went on to be recorded with the London Philharmonic Orchestra.

Lloyd Webber then asked American director Harold Prince to become involved with putting the musical on in the West End. He agreed, but made a few changes including deleting several songs. Its most memorable still remains " Don't Cry For Me Argentina ".

On the 21st of June 1978, Evita opened at the Prince Edward Theatre in the West End. It played for 3176 performances and closed on 18th February 1986, an incredibly popular and successful show.

The lead character was played by Elaine Paige, the parts of Che by David Essex and Peron by Joss Ackland. Evita was nominated for four Olivier Awards, going on to win Best New Musical and Best Performance in a Musical.

In 1979 Evita, opened on Broadway at the Broadway Theatre, with Harold Prince directing and choreography by Larry Fuller. It ran for 1567 performances. Although Elaine Paige was originally booked to recreate her role, she was refused permission on the grounds of being non-American by the Actors Equity Association. In the end, her place was taken by Patti LuPone who moaned that playing the role of Eva was the worst experience of her life, claiming she had no support from her producers and that the music made her suffer from vocal problems. In the end, six actresses played the title role during the run of the show.

However, the production was highly successful and won Best Musical, Best Original Score, Best Book of a Musical, Best Performance by a Leading Actress, Best Direction and Best Lighting at the Tony Awards in 1980. It also won six Drama Desk Awards in the same year, including Outstanding New Musical, Outstanding Lyrics, Outstanding Music, Outstanding Actress, Outstanding Featured Actor and Outstanding Director.

Evita has also become internationally acclaimed and has been produced worldwide, being most popular in Madrid and Brazil.

In 2006, the Adelphi Theatre in London's West End hosted the musical's revival. Athough the reviews were very good, it was not a popular show and the production closed after a run of less than 12 months. Both Philip Quast as Peron and Elena Roger as Eva received Olivier Award nominations for their performances in this revival.

Evita was also revived on Broadway in 2012 at the Marquis Theatre, with the role of Eva being played again by Elena Roger. Ricky Martin played Che and Michael Ceveris was Peron. The musical played for 337 performances and closed 26th January 2013; it was nominated for three Tony awards.

In 1996 Evita was made into a film, directed by Alan Parker with Madonna taking the lead role. The film went on to be a huge success and was nominated for five Academy Awards winning Best Original Song. Although the reviews were mixed for Madonna's performance, she received a Golden Globe Award for Best Actress in a Motion Picture Musical.

Fame

The musical of Fame was based on the hugely successful 1980 feature film directed by Alan Parker which was also followed by a six-season television series in America.

The film's producer David DeSylva changed the format for the musical and wrote an almost entirely new score. The stage show premiered in Miami, Florida in 1988, moving to Philadelphia where it became a sensation at the Walnut Street Theatre in 1989. The musical then toured North America and played in more than 100 cities before moving to off-Broadway in 2003.

Based upon the book by Jose Fernandez, the music was composed by Steve Margoshes and the lyrics were penned by Jacques Levy.

The story of Fame is set in the High School of Performing Arts in New York, following a group of students through the rigors of their lives as they try to become successful performers. The plot is divided into separate sections: auditions to the school, the students' progression through the college and underlying topics such as bullying, sexuality, drugs and friendship.

Fame has been produced in nearly 25 countries and was particularly successful in Stockholm where it ran for nearly four years. Its director/choreographer Runar Borge then stayed with the show and created numerous productions worldwide.

The London production of Fame was nominated for three Laurence Olivier Awards and grossed £56 million at the box office by 2006. It enjoyed seven West End runs in theatres such as the Aldwych Theatre, the Cambridge, the Prince of Wales, the Shaftesbury Theatre, Victoria Palace and went out on numerous tours including a recent run at the new Wimbledon Theatre. Who says Fame doesn't last!

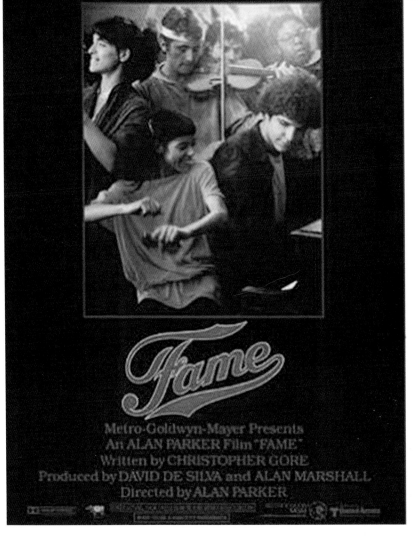

Fiddler on the Roof

Fiddler on the Roof opened on Broadway in 1964 and was the first musical to stage more than 3000 performances holding the record for the longest running Broadway musical for nearly 10 years.

The musical opened at the Imperial Theatre but then transferred to the Majestic Theatre in 1967 then moving to the Broadway Theatre in 1970. Fiddler on the Roof was the last project for famous choreographer and director Jerome Robbins.

To this day, Fiddler on the Roof is still the 16th longest running show in history on Broadway. The show was nominated for 10 Tony awards and won nine of them including Best Musical, Best Score, Best Book, Best Director and Best Choreography.

In 1967, Fiddler on the Roof premiered at her Majesty's Theatre in the West End where it was a huge success, and played for more than 2000 performances. In 1983, the production was revived at the Apollo Theatre and then again at the London Palladium in 1994. It also opened at the Crucible Theatre in Sheffield before moving to the Savoy Theatre, London in May 2007.

The story of Fiddler on the Roof is set in Russia, 1905 in a small Jewish village of Anatevka. It centres around the family of a farmer called Teyve who with his wife Golde and their five daughters battles to cope with their harsh existence under Tsarist rule.

It is based on Tevye and his Daughters (or Tevye the Dairyman) and other tales by Sholem Aleichem which he wrote in Yiddish and published in 1894. The musical's title stems from the painting "The Fiddler" by Marc Chagall, one

of many surreal paintings he created of Eastern European Jewish life, which often included a fiddler, a metaphor for survival, through tradition and joyfulness, in a life of uncertainty and imbalance.

The book was written by Joseph Stein while the music was written by Jerry Bock, with the lyrics by Sheldon Harnick.

In 1971, the musical was adapted for a film, starring Topol (who performed its most famous song, "If I Were a Rich Man") which opened to international acclaim and won three Academy Awards.

The musical endures long lasting success – particularly with schools and amateur societies – and was recently revived in the UK at the Mayflower Theatre in Southampton.

Gentlemen Prefer Blondes

The musical of Gentlemen Prefer Blondes was derived from a best-selling comic novel written by Anita Loos which was first published in the 'Jazz Age' of 1925.

The production of Gentlemen Prefer Blondes was directed by John C Wilson and opened on Broadway in the Ziegfeld Theatre in 1949. The original producers were Herman Levin and Oliver Smith, with Agnes DeMille as the choreographer.

The show was equally successful as the book, and ran until 1951, closing after 740 performances. The title role starred several famous blonde actresses over the years, including Jayne Mansfield, Betty Hutton and Barbara Eden.

The story of Gentlemen Prefer Blondes follows the lives of Miss Lorelei Lee – whose believes that "diamonds are a girl's best friend" – and her best friend Dorothy.

The girls embark on a boat trip to Paris, where Miss Lee intends to marry a millionaire called Gus Esmond. However, en route, the girls are spied on by private detective Malone who has been hired by Esmond's father to make sure that she isn't just another gold digger.

When Dorothy falls in love with the poverty stricken Malone, Lorelei decides to find her friend a wealthier potential husband, and she gets mixed up with a flirtatious diamond merchant. The story ends well though, with a double wedding for both Lorelei and Dorothy.

The film adaptation of the musical was produced in 1953, famously starring Marilyn Monroe with Jane Russell. The film opened to rave reviews from both critics and audiences, and became one of the highest grossing films of 1953 earning

The PLAYBILL for the Ziegfeld Theatre

Gentlemen Prefer Blondes

more than $7.5 million dollars at the box office.

The scene in which Monroe sings "Diamonds Are a Girl's Best Friend" is one of the most iconic in the history of screen musicals.

In 1962, the stage revival opened at the Princess Theatre in London's West End running for 223 performances, featuring Dora Bryan as Lorelei Lee.

A version entitled Lorelei, opened on Broadway at the Palace Theatre in 1974, running for 320 performances, starring Carol Channing who received a Tony Award nomination for Best Actress in a Musical.

The show has subsequently been revived on Broadway and in London during the 1990s with mixed success – having a hard act to follow in living up to the long-lasting appeal of the star-studded film.

Gigi

The story of Gigi was written by famous French author Sidonie-Gabrielle Colette in Paris, in 1945.

Six years later, Gigi was produced as a play on Broadway by Gilbert Miller. It starred Audrey Hepburn making her Broadway debut and opened to critical acclaim.

In 1958, the novella was turned into an Oscar winning hit musical film which featured songs written by Alan Jay Lerner. The music was written by Frederik Loewe and it was arranged and conducted by Andre Previn. The film starred Maurice Chevalier and Louis Jourdan Gaston.

The story is based upon a young 18th century Parisien girl named Gigi who lives with her mother and grandmother. In the home of her aunt, she is given lessons in social manners, conversation and personal relationships and is being groomed for a career as a courtesan.

The family have many good social connections and are friends with rich playboy Gaston who is bored with his life, however he seems to take great delight in being in the company of Gigi and her family.

When Gigi's aunt deems that the time is right for her to enter society, she presents Gigi as an accomplished young woman to Gaston who is unhappy at the change in her. Gradually, however he sees Gigi in a new light. He falls in love with her and proposes marriage which she gladly accepts.

In 1973 Gigi was finally adapted as a Broadway musical but sadly the debut failed to live up to the success of the film. It only ran for 103 performances but managed to win a Tony Award for Best Score.

ALFRED DRAKE   AGNES MOOREHEAD
MARIA KARNILOVA
and
DANIEL MASSEY
in
Lerner and Loewe's

Gigi

with
KARIN WOLFE as Gigi

RCA VICTOR

The musical went on to be produced in at the Lyric Theatre in London's West End and ran for only seven months. However, in 2008 a new production of Gigi was premiered at Regent's Park Open Air Theatre and became one of the biggest shows of the season.

There are plans for a revival of Gigi in a pre-Broadway production at the Kennedy Centre in January 2015. It will be directed by Eric Schaeffer and will then be hoping for a Broadway run in 2015.

Grease

The musical Grease was first performed at the Kingston Mines Theatre in Chicago in 1971 having been created by Jim Jacobs and Warren Casey.

However, just a few months later in February 1972, it moved off Broadway to the Eden Theatre in Manhattan. This created some controversy, as it was not eligible for the Tony Awards with the committee deeming that the Eden did not qualify as a Broadway theatre. The producers threatened to sue and the committee promptly backed down.

Their confidence in the show was vindicated and Grease received seven Tony nominations and promptly moved to The Broadhurst Theatre, Broadway in June 1972. It then transferred to the Royale Theatre where it ran until January 1980, closing at the larger Majestic Theatre for the last five weeks of its run.

The musical was an undeniable smash hit and by the time it closed in April 1980, it had run for more than 3000 performances. It still remains the 15th longest running show on Broadway.

Many famous actors were included in the Broadway casts including the likes of Patrick Swayze, John Travolta and Richard Gere, who was understudy for many of the lead roles in this production.

The musical follows the story of ten working-class teenagers at a fictional American high school in 1959 with the songs reflecting the sexual tension of the burgeoning rock and roll age.

In 1973, the production opened at the New London Theatre in the West End. Both Paul Nicholas and Elaine Paige starred in the production and the cast also included the then unknown Richard Gere as Danny.

John Travolta went on to star in the blockbuster film of the same name in 1978 playing the character Danny Zuko, although interestingly, he played the character Doody who worshipped the more popular character Danny in the 1972 tour across the US and Canada. The scene he played opposite Olivia Newton John (clad from top to toe in black leather) singing, "You're The One That I Want" remains one of the most sexually charged dance sequences in the history of screen musicals.

The stage musical struck a universal chord everywhere it opened, with a highly irresistible mix of vibrant physicality, adolescent angst and 1950s pop culture. In 1993, a new production of Grease which incorporated all the hit songs from the movie opened at the Dominion Theatre and starred Craig MacLachlan as Danny Zuko. This production remained very popular and was taken on tour starring both Shane Ritchie and then Ian Kelsey as the main character. The production finished after six very successful years in 1999 whilst the tour carried on throughout the UK.

Another UK tour took place in 2004. The show broke the box office record in Sunderland, previously held by Cats;

had the highest one week capacity at the Royal Concert Hall in Nottingham; and sold out in Bristol seven weeks before its arrival. In Edinburgh, Grease also sold out before its arrival, the only other show to do so being Showboat 12 years previously.

Grease still enjoys frequent revivals around the world and is currently touring in Australia where it will be performed in Melbourne, Perth and Adelaide, proving it's the one that audiences want!

Above: *The original Broadway Cast album*

Guys and Dolls

Guys and Dolls was based on two Damon Runyon books entitled "The Idyll of Miss Sarah Brown" and "Blood Pressure" with parts of its plot, characters and story also borrowed from Runyon's "Pick the Winner."

The lyrics and music were written by the legendary Frank Loesser with the critics unanimous in their praise, most agreeing that the songs fitted the storyline with great sensitivity.

The story of Guys and Dolls is set in the 1950s in New York's Times Square in the twilight world of gangsters and their molls. More a musical fable of Broadway, the characters very vividly drawn, some of them street wise and some of them furiously funny.

In 1950, Guys and Dolls, directed by George S Kaufmann, premiered on Broadway at 46th Theatre. It opened to rave reviews and went on to run for more than 1200 performances. In 1951, Guys and Dolls was nominated for and won five Tony Awards including Best Musical and Best Book.

The musical went on to open in London's West End at the London Coliseum in 1953. It was equally successful here, running for 555 performances. Frank Loesser interestingly only chose one British actor (Lizbeth Webb) for a starring role in the original London production, the rest being American.

Two years later it was released on the silver screen starring Marlon Brando, Jean Simmons, Frank Sinatra and Vivian Blaine. The film was very successful, grossing over $20 million at the box office, and was nominated for four Academy Awards and two Golden Globes which it won.

A DECCA BROADWAY ORIGINAL CAST ALBUM

FEUER and MARTIN present

GUYS & DOLLS

A MUSICAL FABLE of BROADWAY

Based on a story and characters by DAMON RUNYON

starring

ROBERT ALDA · VIVIAN BLAINE · SAM LEVENE

ISABEL BIGLEY · PAT ROONEY, Sr.

B. S. PULLY · STUBBY KAYE · TOM PEDI · JOHNNY SILVER

Music and Lyrics by FRANK LOESSER

Book by JO SWERLING and ABE BURROWS

Directed by GEORGE S. KAUFMAN

DECCA BROADWAY

The 1982 London musical revival won actor Bob Hoskins, as Nathan Detroit, a Critics Circle Theatre Award, with the production itself winning five Olivier Awards including one for actress Julia McKenzie and also one for Best Musical.

The show has gone on to be revived countless times internationally, most recently in the UK at the Chichester Festival Theatre during their 2014 season.

Above: *Original cast album*

Hairspray

Based on the 1988 film by John Waters, the musical Hairspray has enjoyed huge international success particularly on Broadway and in the West End.

Hairspray originated from a book written by Mark O'Donnell and Thomas Meehan. The story is set in 1962 and tells of a plump young girl from Baltimore who is passionate about dance. She wins a spot on the local television dance program and changes from being an outsider to an irrepressible teen celebrity.

In 2002, the musical had a successful trial in Seattle at the 5th Avenue Theatre and went on to open at the Neil Simon Theatre on Broadway in August of the same year. The show was infamous for its fabulous wigs, made by Paul Huntley. The lyrics for Hairspray were written by Marc Shaiman and Scott Wittman, with Shaiman also writing the music for the production. The show ran for 2,642 performances, a total of six years on Broadway.

Although Hairspray initially received a mixed review from the critics, it was nominated for 12 Tony Awards and won eight of them including those for Best Musical, Best Book, Best Score and Best Direction.

In 2007, Hairspray opened at the Shaftesbury Theatre in London's West End. The original team from the Broadway production, including director Jack O'Brien and choreographer Jerry Mitchell, came to London to produce the show. The musical set a record, being nominated for 11 Olivier Awards, winning Best New Musical and also Best Actress and Actor in a Musical for Leanne Jones and Michael Ball.

BROADWAY'S BIG FAT MUSICAL COMEDY HIT

In the same year, Hairspray was made into a blockbuster film starring John Travolta, Michelle Pfeiffer, Queen Latifah and Zach Efron, grossing a hair-raising $200 million at the box office.

The stage show has been revived many times internationally including a tour of the UK in 2014.

Hello, Dolly!

Hello, Dolly! is one of the most popular and best-loved American musicals of all time

It was originally based upon a 1835 English play called A Day Well Spent by John Oxenford, this was then turned into a farce by Johann Nestroy, which in turn became a book written by Michael Stewart. In later years it was renamed, The Matchmaker and was based upon Thornton Wilder's farce named the Merchant of Yonkers.

The story is based upon the character of Dolly Levi, the New York-based matchmaker who merrily arranges things, anything from furniture and daffodils to other people's lives. A widow herself, she finds herself in love with a Yonkers merchant and proceeds to weave a web of romantic complications involving both him, his two clerks, a pretty milliner and her assistant.

The show premiered at the St James Theatre on Broadway in 1964 and remained there until 1970 running for a total of 2844 performances. It was produced by David Merrick with Gower Champion directing and choreographing.

Although facing stiff competition from the hit musical Funny Girl, starring Barbra Streisand, Hello, Dolly! swept up at the Tony awards in 1964 winning 10 out of its 11 nominations.

Famously, the role of Dolly Levi was originally written for Ethel Merman who turned it down, as did Mary Martin, although both actresses eventually went on to play the part.

The production received rave reviews, and became the longest running musical and third longest running show on Broadway, beating My Fair Lady.

It was only surpassed by Fiddler on the Roof and then Grease. Hello, Dolly! was a phenomenal hit, grossing $27 million at the box office.

In 1965, the musical was premiered at the Theatre Royal, Drury Lane in the West End. Gower Champion was brought to the UK to direct and choreograph, and the show ran for 794 performances, starring Mary Martin as Dolly.

The show has enjoyed many revivals including three in London's West End. The London production in 2010 was nominated for three Laurence Olivier Awards and won Best Musical Revival, Best Actress in a Musical for Samantha Spiro and Best Theatre Choreographer for Stephen Mear.

In 1969, Hello, Dolly! was made into a musical film, directed by Gene Kelly and adapted and produced by Ernest Lehman. The film starred Walter Matthau in his only musical movie, alongside the likes of Barbra Streisand, Michael Crawford and Louis Armstrong who had recorded the title tune which had gone on to top the charts in May 1964. The film won three Acadamy Awards although had been nominated for four others. Despite having good success at the box office, grossing $33.2 million in the United States alone, the film is reckoned to have lost its backers an estimated $10 million. Bye, Bye, Dollars!

Charles the Second

Theatre Royal Drury Lane

MARY MARTIN

in

HELLO, DOLLY!

This design is copied from the original Charter granted by King Charles II to Thomas Killigrew in 1663 the original document is still in existence.

PROGRAMME — ONE SHILLING

Jersey Boys

After the success of Buddy and Mamma Mia!, both based around rock and pop soundtracks, the producers of Jersey Boys were confident that they could have similar success with the songs of the Four Seasons.

Indeed, it was Bob Gaudio, one of the original members of the band, who was one of the motivating forces behind the creation of the show.

He enlisted the help of producer Bob Crewe and the writers of the original Jersey Boys book, Marshall Brickman and Rick Elice, to put together a jukebox style musical about the band's history.

Brickman was drawn to the project because: "It's a classic American story. Rag's to riches and back to rags!"

The writers gathered material from interviews with the surviving Four Seasons' members Gaudio, Frankie Valli and Tommy DeVito. Of the three, they approached DeVito last who told them: " Don't listen to those guys. I'll tell you what really happened. "

The end result was the musical biography of the Four Seasons and the rise, the tough times and the personal clashes with the ultimate triumph of a group of friends whose music was to become symbolic of their generation.

The production was more than a mere tribute concert and although it included many numbers from the Four Seasons song book, Jersey Boys got to the heart of the relationships within the group with special focus on front man Frankie Valli.

The core of the show highlighted how an allegiance to a code of honour which was learned in the streets of their native New Jersey managed to get them through a multitude of challenges including gambling,

debts, Mafia threats and family disasters.

Jersey Boys officially opened on Broadway at the August Wilson Theatre in November 2005. It was a huge success and has now played for more than 3000 performances, becoming the 14th longest running show on Broadway. The musical has gone on to tour the United States, playing in 38 cities.

In 2008, Jersey Boys debuted at the Prince Edward Theatre in London's West End. Here again it was critically acclaimed, winning the Laurence Olivier Award for Best New Musical. In March 2004, the production moved to the Picadilly Theatre and is due to run for another year. Star of the show. Ryan Molloy played Frankie Valli for more than six years, making him the longest running star in a West End musical.

A national tour of the UK is planned for Autumn 2014, opening at the Palace Theatre in Manchester, while the story has also been made into a feature film directed by Clint Eastwood which was released in 2014.

Jesus Christ Superstar

Jesus Christ Superstar was more of rock opera than a traditional musical and helped launch the meteoric careers of creators Andrew Lloyd Webber and Tim Rice

First staged on Broadway in 1971, it was loosely based on the life of Jesus as portrayed in the Gospels, beginning with his arrival with his disciples into Jerusalem and ending with his crucifixion. The storyline also highlighted the political and personal struggles between Judas Iscariot and Jesus that were not portrayed in the Bible.

Jesus Christ Superstar was originally produced as an album, with the part of Jesus being sung by Ian Gillan, the lead singer of Deep Purple, and that of Judas by Murray Head. The future Gary Glitter had a one-liner as a priest and Michael d'Abo appeared as King Herod. The title song, "Superstar", sung by Judas (Head), and "I Don't Know How to Love Him", sung by Mary Magdalene (Yvonne Elliman) about her relationship with Jesus, were both big hits.

The original album had a rock flavour that was very different from Lloyd Webber's later work. This was in part due to the emotive singing of Head and Gillan and the playing of well-known rock session musicians such as guitarists Neil Hubbard and Chris Spedding, bassist Alan Spenner and drummer Bruce Rowland.

On April 4, 1971, the musical was presented for the first time in a live concert performance by the Ravenswood Rock Group, sponsored by the Bel Canto Opera at New York's Madison Avenue Baptist Church.

In June of that year, the first staged version was performed by students

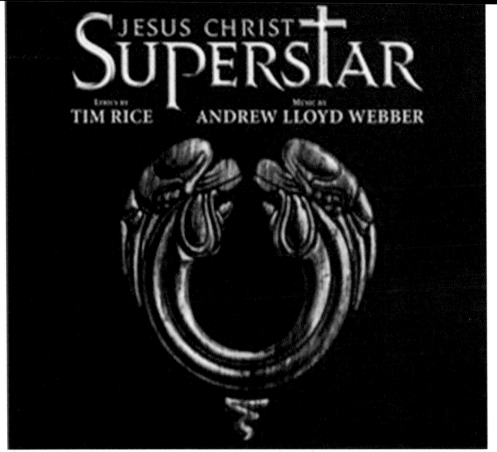

JESUS CHRIST SUPERSTAR

Lyrics by
TIM RICE

Music by
ANDREW LLOYD WEBBER

at Southold High School in New York. However, other unauthorized productions were also going on at the time, eliciting lawsuits from the authors which eventually resulted in the shutting-down of several hundred productions before the official premiere. (This injunction became a benchmark in copyright law).

On July 11, 1971, the first authorized

American concert took place in front of an audience of 13,000 people at Pittsburgh, Pennsylvania's Civic Arena with Jeff Fenholt singing the role of Jesus, Carl Anderson as Judas, and Yvonne Elliman as Mary Magdalene.

The musical finally opened on Broadway on October 12, 1971, directed by Tom O'Horgan, at the Mark Hellinger Theatre, to mixed reviews with critics from The New York Times deeming it to be a heartless over-hyped production. The show closed on June 30, 1973 after just 711 performances.

The Broadway show and subsequent productions were condemned by some religious groups. Tim Rice was quoted as saying "It happens that we don't see Christ as God but simply the right man at the right time at the right place."

Some Christians considered these comments to be blasphemous, the character of Judas too sympathetic and some of his criticisms of Jesus offensive. At the same time, some Jews claimed that it bolstered the anti-semitic belief that the Jews were responsible for Jesus's death by showing most of the villains as Jewish and showing the crowd in Jerusalem calling for the crucifixion. The musical was banned in South Africa for being "irreligious".

Despite this controversy it opened at the Palace Theatre in London's West End in 1972 starring Paul Nicholas as Jesus, Stephen Tate as Judas and Dana Gillespie as Mary.

The production in London was much more successful than its counterpart in New York, running for eight years which at that time became Britain's longest running musical. Even now, it is the 17th longest running show to ever be staged on the West End.

In 1973, Jesus Christ Superstar was directed as a film by Norman Jewison and quickly became one of the top ten highest grossing films of the year and was nominated for several Golden Globe Awards.

The stage show has continued to enjoy huge longevity and success. The 1980 production in London's West End grossed over £7.5 million running for 3358 performances.

In 2000, Jesus Christ Superstar was even endorsed by the Vatican and songs from the show were performed in front of the Pope John Paul II in Rome. It is reckoned that since its inception, the musical has now grossed more than £120 million and has been shown in more than 40 countries.

Joseph and the Amazing Technicolor Dreamcoat

Joseph and the Amazing Technicolor Dreamcoat was the first musical written by Tim Rice and Andrew Lloyd Webber ever to be publicly performed.

The show, based on the "coat of many colors" story of Joseph from the Bible's Book of Genesis, was originally performed as a 15-minute pop cantata in 1968 at the Colet School in London and was subsequently recorded as a concept album in 1969.

It was Andrew Lloyd Webber's father, himself a composer, who encouraged and arranged for a second performance as he felt that the show had huge talent in the making. The second performance was at his local church, Westminster Central Hall and received positive reviews by The Sunday Times. It went on to be performed at St Paul's Cathedral in November 1968 but still only had a running time of 35 minutes.

In the meantime, Lloyd Webber and Rice had released their second musical, Jesus Christ Superstar which was becoming popular in America. Encouraged by this growing success they decided to produce Joseph at the Cathedral College of the Immaculate Conception in New York 1970.

Joseph was presented at the Edinburgh International Festival by the Young Vic Theatre Company, directed by Frank Dunlop. It then moved to London's Young Vic Theatre in October 1970 and then on to the Roundhouse Theatre.

Finally in February 1973, the musical was produced at the Alderbury Theatre in London's West End where it ran for 243 performances.

After a fairly rocky start, with some productions off-Broadway, the musical

finally opened at Broadways Royale Theatre in 1982 to huge success and ran for 747 performances. The show was both directed and choreographed by Tony Tanner and was nominated for several Tony awards, including Best Musical and Best Original Score. The starring role of Joseph was taken by David Cassidy (famous as a teen heart-throb at the time) in March 1983.

When the show re-opened at the London Palladium in 1991, actor Jason Donovan took the starring role with Stephen Pimlott, the director. This performance was a huge success and when Donovan left, the former children's television presenter Philip Schofield came in to play the part of Joseph. In 1990, the musical won a Laurence Olivier Award for the song "Any Dream Will Do" which topped the British charts for two weeks between June and July 1991.

The show has had many successful revivals. In 2007 Joseph opened at the Adelphi Theatre and became the subject of a BBC One talent search series to find a new leading man to play the lead role. The tickets for the show sold out so fast that it took just three weeks to sell all the tickets allocated for the first three months. The producers extended the show's run having rumoured to have banked over £10 million in advanced ticket sales. Andrew Lloyd Webber donated all receipts from two special performances of the show to the BBC's Children In Need charity appeal.

Joseph has now been performed by both professional and amateur companies all over the world and by thousands of schools. It is the first professional production that incorporates a children's choir as an integral part of the production and so far has grossed a dreamy £400 million.

Les Misérables

Les Miserables is the most successful British musical of all time, seen by more than 65 million people in 42 countries and in 22 languages around the globe.

Set against the backdrop of 19th-century France, 'Les Mis' – as it is more commonly known - tells the enthralling story of ex-convict Jean Valjean who is hunted for decades by the ruthless policeman Javert after he breaks parole. When Valjean agrees to care for factory worker Fantine's young daughter, Cosette, their lives change forever.

The sentimental plot almost plays second fiddle to the music of Claude-Michel Schönberg, the lyrics of Alain Boublil and Jean-Marc Natel and an English-language libretto by Herbert Kretzmer. Featuring the songs "I Dreamed A Dream", "Bring Him Home", "One Day More" and "On My Own" – it is often hailed as the show of shows.

It is currently the longest-running musical in the West End, closely followed by The Phantom of the Opera. In January 2010, it celebrated its 10,000th performance in the Queen's Theatre in London's West End. On the 3rd of October 2010, the show celebrated its 25th anniversary with three productions running in the same city: the original show at the Queen's Theatre; the 25th Anniversary touring production at the original home of the show, the Barbican Centre; and the 25th Anniversary concert at London's O2 Arena.

The Broadway production opened on the 12th of March 1987 and ran until the 18th of May 2003, closing after 6,680 performances. It is the third longest-

running Broadway show in history. A fully re-orchestrated Broadway revival opened on November the 9th 2006 at the Broadhurst Theatre.

The show was nominated for 12 Tony Awards, winning eight, including Best Musical and Best Original Score. Les Misérables was placed first in a BBC Radio 2 listener poll of the "Nation's Number One Essential Musicals" in June 2005, receiving more than 40% of the votes cast.

The musical's famous emblem is a cropped head-and-shoulders portrait of Cosette superimposed on the French national flag. The picture is based on the

Opposite: *The set from the 2012 film adaptation of Les Misérables*

illustration by Émile Bayard that appeared in the original edition of the novel in 1862.

French songwriter Alain Boublil decided to adapt Victor Hugo's novel into a musical while watching a performance of the musical Oliver! in London. He proposed the idea to French composer Claude-Michel Schönberg, and they developed a rough synopsis of what they believed would work in a musical. They made an analysis of each character's mental and emotional state, as well as that of the audience watching the show.

After two years of hard work, a two-hour demo tape with Schönberg accompanying himself on the piano and singing the role of each character was finally completed. An album of this collaboration was recorded at CTS Studios in Wembley and released in 1980, selling 260,000 copies.

The English language version, with lyrics supplied by Herbert Kretzmer and additional material by James Fenton, was expanded and reworked from a literal translation by Siobhan Bracke of the original Paris version.

The first production of Les Miserables in English was produced by Cameron Mackintosh and then adapted and directed by Trevor Nunn and John Caird, opening on the 8th of October 1985 (this was five years after the original production) at the Barbican Arts Centre in London.

The set for the show was designed by John Napier, the costumes by Andreane Neofitou and the lighting by David Hersey. The musical supervision and orchestrations were by John Cameron with the staging by Kate Flatt and the musical direction by Martin Koch.

The production starred Colm Wilkinson as Jean Valjean, Frances Ruffelle as Éponine, Rebecca Caine as Cosette, Patti LuPone as Fantine, Roger Allam as the persistent Inspector Javert, Michael Ball as Marius, Zoe Hart as young Cosette, Susan Jane Tanner as Madame Thénardier, David Burt as Enjolras, Ian Tucker and Oliver Spencer as Gavroche, and Alun Armstrong as the villainous, but funny rogue Thénardier.

On the 4th December 1985, the show finally transferred to the Palace Theatre, London but moved again on the 3rd of April 2004, to the smaller Queen's Theatre, with a few revisions for the staging and where it is still playing

Incredibly, Peter Boita, the original drummer, is still with the show – the musical equivalent of the Duracell bunny!

Little Shop of Horrors

Little Shop of Horrors is a musical based upon the 1960s black comedy film directed by Roger Corman.

The farcical story concerns an inadequate florist's assistant who cultivates a plant that feeds on human flesh and blood.

The cult B-movie was the inspiration for the comedy horror rock musical, which was written by Howard Ashman. The style of music, composed by Alan Menken, was very much 1960's rock 'n' roll, doo-wop and early Motown.

The musical opened off-Broadway at the Orpheum Theatre in 1982 and was directed by Ashman with the staging by Eddie Callan. The production was well received by the critics and won many awards including New York Drama Critics' Circle Award for Best Musical, the Drama Desk Award for Outstanding Musical, and the Outer Critics' Circle Award.

The Little Shop of Horrors went on to run for five years, closing in 1987 after 2209 performances. It was then the third longest running musical and the highest grossing production in off-Broadway history.

The West End production opened in 1983 at the Comedy Theatre. It was produced by Cameron Mackintosh and ran for 813 performances. The show received the Evening Standard Award for Best Musical and closed in 1985.

In 1986, a film version of the musical was made, directed by Frank Oz. The tragic ending (when the plant eats the store assistant) had been changed to a more upbeat one, but the original was restored in the directors cut of the film in October 2012. The film received one

Left: *Album cover*

Academy Award for Best Original Song.

There have been several subsequent productions of the musical. A revival was planned in 2003 on Broadway, but the show opened to mixed reviews. After a few changes, the producers decided to cancel the production. However, veteran Broadway director Jerry Zaks was brought in and the musical made its debut at the Virginia Theatre on Broadway in October 2003. It was nominated for one Tony Award, the category being the Best Actor in a Musical.

The revival in London was directed by Matthew White in 2006 and became a critical and commercial success, transferring to the Duke of York's Theatre in London's West End in March 2007, transferring once more to the Ambassadors Theatre and being nominated for a Laurence Olivier Award in 2008.

Me and My Girl

If ever a musical has stood the test of time it is Me and My Girl.

The original show was first performed in London's West End in 1937 at the West End Victoria Palace Theatre, starring Lupino Lane, and it was still being performed in London some 70 years later!

The music was written by Noel Gay and the original book and lyrics were by Douglas Furber and L. Arthur Rose. The show is famous for its song "The Lambeth Walk."

The production originally attracted very little notice, but after being broadcast live on BBC Radio (this only occurred as there was a cancellation of a sporting event) the show gained more success and the performance went on to be televised from the theatre in 1939. The original West End production ran for 1646 performances.

The story of Me and My Girl revolves around a rather unrefined cockney gentleman called Bill who learns that he is the 14th Earl of Hareford. However, he discovers that he will only receive his inheritance if Sir John and the Duchess approve of him. The Duchess feels that with a little grooming, Bill will be suitable to inherit the title and the money but she insists that Bill has to break up with his cockney girlfriend named Sally. Bill refuses to accept the title if he cannot keep Sally as his girl. Eventually, Sally is groomed to become more ladylike and Bill is allowed to inherit the title and to keep his girl.

Me and My Girl has been revived on many occasions, most notably in 1952 and then again in 1984. This production opened at the Leicester Haymarket Theatre. The script had been revised by Stephen Fry and Mike Ockrent. It opened to very good reviews and was transferred to the Adelphi Theatre in 1985, closing in 1993 with an eight year run and 3303 performances. Stars such as Robert Lindsay, Emma Thompson and Frank Thornton were involved in the production.

Me and My Girl won two Olivier Awards for Musical of the Year and Outstanding Performance of an Actor in a Musical (Robert Lindsay)

After the production in London, the musical subsequently toured throughout Britain and has been staged all across the UK over the years. In 1997, it appeared at the Royal Shakespeare Theatre for a limited run.

In 1986 Me and My Girl opened on Broadway at the Marquis Theatre where it ran for 1420 performances and closed in December 1989. This production was very successful, being nominated for 13 Tony awards and winning four for Best Actor (Lindsay), Best Actress (Maryann Plunkett) and Best Choreographer (Gillian Gregory).

In 2006, a 70th anniversary production of Me and My Girl ran for an eight month British tour, this was directed and choreographed by Warren Carlyle with

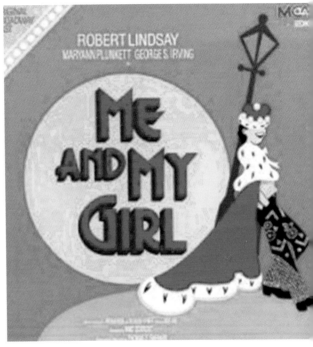

the cast including Richard Frame, Faye Tozer and Sylvester McCoy.

Sadly in 2010 the revival of Me and My Girl which was staged at the Crucible Theatre in Sheffield had to be scrapped, when the expected transfer to London's West End didn't come to fruition as no theatre was available.

Above: *Original Broadway cast recording*

Miss Saigon

Miss Saigon was the brainchild of Claude-Michel Schonberg and Alain Boubil who had both formerly been involved with the writing of Les Miserables.

The musical was inspired by a photograph showing a Vietnamese mother leaving her child to be collected at the departure gate by her ex GI father in Vietnam; it is a story similar to Puccinis's famous opera Madam Butterfly.

The musical is based in Saigon during the last weeks of the Vietnam war in April 1975. It tells the story of a young GI called Chris who meets 17-year-old Kim in a nightclub. They fall in love but when Chris has to leave the city in a hurry in a helicopter, he leaves Kim behind without sending any message to her. After three years, Chris marries an American girl and builds a new life but cannot forget Kim.

Kim bore a child and was living under the tyrannical dictatorship of Ho Chi Minh. She has never forgotten Chris, who knows nothing of his son and she refuses the affection of Officer Thuy to whom she was promised as a wife since her childhood. In a rage Officer Thuys tries to kill Kim's son and in his defence, she shoots him, escaping to her brother in Bangkok. Chris then finds out that he had a child by Kim and tries to find them. Together with his wife they fly to Thailand, Kim discovers the arrival of Chris and goes to his hotel. There, however, she meets his wife and discovers the truth of his new life in America.

The original musical of Miss Saigon was the first premiered at the Theatre Royal, Drury Lane, in London's West End in 1989. It ran for 10 years and enjoyed over 4000 performances. The production was

directed by Nicolas Hytner with musical staging by Bob Avian, the scenic design was by John Napier. In December 1994, this production became the Theatre Royal's longest running musical and eclipsed the record set by My Fair Lady.

In 1991, Miss Saigon debuted at the Broadway Theatre on Broadway and ran for 4092 performances, closing in January 2001. The British production team, Nicolas Hytner, Bob Avian and John Napier were brought over to America for this production and can take great credit that Miss Saigon is still one of the longest running Broadway musicals in musical theatre history.

Indeed, the show on Broadway broke the record for advanced ticket sales at $24 million – with the highest priced tickets at $100 - and repaid its investors in fewer than 39 weeks.

The show has enjoyed successes worldwide and has been particularly popular touring the UK and US. It has now played in 300 cities and in 15 different languages, winning awards around the world.

Miss Saigon has not been without its criticisms. There were several cries of racism as white actors playing Asian characters were seen to be wearing eye prostheses and bronzing creams to make themselves appear more Asian.

In England, Miss Saigon was nominated for four Laurence Olivier Awards in 1989, winning Best Actor in a Musical for Jonathan Pryce and Best Actress in a Musical for Lea Salonga. However, it missed out for Best Musical to Return to the Forbidden Planet.

In America, the production was nominated 11 times for the Tony Awards in 1991, winning Best Performance by a Leading Actor in a Musical and Best Performance by a Leading Actress in a Musical for the duo who had played the roles in London.

Cameron Mackintosh is producing the revival of Miss Saigon at the Prince Edward theatre in London's West End in 2014.

My Fair Lady

My Fair Lady, based upon the book Pygmalion by George Bernard Shaw, is often considered to be the greatest musical of all time.

With lyrics by Alan Jay Lerner and music by Frederik Loewe, the show contains numerous classic songs including Wouldn't It Be Loverly, With a Little Bit of Luck, Just You Wait, The Rain in Spain, I Could Have Danced All Night, On The Street Where You Live, Get Me To The Church on Time and I've Grown Accustomed to Her Face – tunes that can be instantly recalled by generations of theatergoers.

The charming story centres around Henry Higgins who is a Professor of Phonetics. He encounters Eliza Doolittle, a Cockney flower girl at the Covent Garden market and declares to his friend Colonel Pickering that in three months

he could transform Eliza into a Duchess.

Eliza is moved into the Higgins household and put through a grueling course of phonetics and elocution lessons. Her moment of triumph comes at the embassy ball where she looks beautiful, is elegant and well spoken and proves to be a huge hit. After the ball, Eliza is despondent as she sees Higgins celebrating his triumph without showing consideration for her feelings. Unnoticed, she leaves the Higgins house and seeks refuge with his mother. Higgins comes in search of her but Eliza refuses to return with him. Once back home Higgins realizes he has become 'accustomed' to Eliza, and the show ends on a happy note when she reappears and forgives him.

It was film producer Gabriel Pascal who acquired the rights to produce the film versions of Shaw's plays including

Music by Frederick Loewe
Lyrics by Alan Jay Lerner

Pygmalion. However, the celebrated author refused permission for Pygmalion to be adapted into a musical and it wasn't until Shaw died in 1950 that Pascal asked Alan Jay Lerner to write the musical adaptation.

Interestingly, both Rodgers and Hammerstein had given up trying to adapt Pygmalion into a musical and had told Lerner and Loewe that converting the play into a musical would be impossible. Disheartened, they abandoned the project for two years.

On the death of Pascal, Lerner and Loewe reunited and realised that the play would only need a few changes to turn it into a successful musical.

The musical was credited for discovering young British actress Julie Andrews and although Noel Coward was first to be offered the role of Henry Higgins, he turned it down, suggesting that the producers cast Rex Harrison instead.

The musical had its pre-Broadway try-out at New Haven's Shubert Theatre but nearly ended before it had begun. On opening night Harrison, who was unaccustomed to singing in front of a live orchestra, announced that under no circumstances would he go on that night... " with those 32 interlopers in the pit". He locked himself in his dressing room and came out little more than an hour before curtain time. The whole company had been dismissed but were recalled, and opening night proved a sensation.

In 1956, the musical opened on Broadway at the Mark Hellinger Theatre, transferring to the Broadhurst Theatre and then to the Broadway Theatre in 1962.

My Fair Lady played for a record 2717 performances, and was directed by Moss Hart with the choreographer being Hanya Holm.

The Broadway show was showered with awards and moved to London's West End in 1958 opening at the Theatre Royal, Drury Lane where it was equally successful, running for more than five years and 2281 performances.

In 1964, the Oscar winning film version of My Fair Lady, directed by George Cukor, opened to rave reviews although it was not without its controversies as Audrey Hepburn was cast in the role of Eliza instead of Julie Andrews.

Most theatregoers had regarded Andrews as perfect for the part and were

equally upset that Hepburn's singing voice was dubbed by Marnie Nixon. However, justice was done when Andrews won the Oscar over Hepburn for her role in Mary Poppins in the same year.

A new revival of My Fair Lady was planned for 2014 with the production possibly starting at the Sheffield Crucible before moving to the West End. Both Dominic West and Carly Bawden were asked to star in the roles of Henry Higgins and Eliza.

Oklahoma!

Oklahoma! was the first musical to be written by famous duo of composer Richard Rodgers and librettist Oscar Hammerstein.

Based on Lynn Riggs' 1931 play Green Grow the Lilacs set in Oklahoma, the musical tells the story of Laurey Williams and Curly, the handsome shy ranch hand who has been acting strangely around her.

She and Curly soon realise that they have feelings for each other but he has a rival in Judd, a hired hand at Laurey's home. Together, she and Curly have to do something to save their relationship and keep Judd from doing something terrible.

A sub-plot features Ado Annie, one of Laurey's friends, whose boyfriend has just come back from a trip to Kansas City. Whilst he was away, she has fallen in love with a peddlar who is a ladies man and doesn't really want to marry her. The question begs does she stay with her boyfriend or run away with a peddlar?

Set against the backdrop of ranching, Oklahoma! the musical is full of fun, music and romance for everyone.

Oklahoma! opened in 1943 at the St James's Theatre on Broadway. It was an immediate box office smash hit and ran for 2212 performances, winning both Rodgers and Hammerstein a special Pulitzer Prize in 1944.

In post war Britain, Oklahoma! was one of the first Broadway musicals to reach London's West End. It opened at the Theatre Royal, Drury Lane in 1947 starring Howard Keele and Betty Jane Watson. The show had rave press reviews and many sell-outs running for 1543 performances.

In 1955, Oklahoma! was successfully

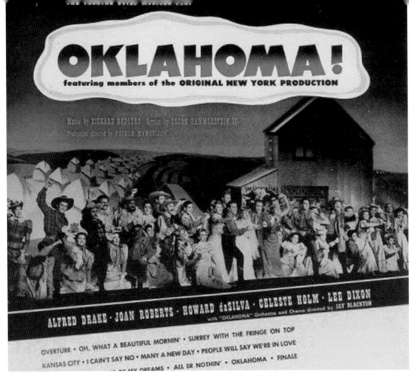

OKLAHOMA!

featuring members of the ORIGINAL NEW YORK PRODUCTION

Music by RICHARD RODGERS · Lyrics by OSCAR HAMMERSTEIN II
Production directed by OSCAR HAMMERSTEIN

ALFRED DRAKE · JOAN ROBERTS · HOWARD deSILVA · CELESTE HOLM · LEE DIXON
with "OKLAHOMA" Orchestra and Chorus directed by JAY BLACKTON

OVERTURE · OH, WHAT A BEAUTIFUL MORNIN' · SURREY WITH THE FRINGE ON TOP
KANSAS CITY · I CAIN'T SAY NO · MANY A NEW DAY · PEOPLE WILL SAY WE'RE IN LOVE
... MY DREAMS · ALL ER NOTHIN' · OKLAHOMA · FINALE

adapted for film. Rodgers and Hammerstein were involved in the production to prevent the studio from making too many changes from the stage version. The film won Academy Awards for Best Music, Scoring of a Musical Picture and Best Sound Recording.

Oklahoma! has enjoyed many revivals on both Broadway and in the West End. In the 1980 and 1998 West End revivals, producers Cameron Mackintosh and Trevor Nunn were both involved with award winning productions of the show.

Oklahoma! is probably the most important of the Rogers and Hammerstein musicals, as it was the first fully integrated musical play, blending songs, character, plot and even dance that would serve as a model for Broadway shows for decades to come.

Oliver!

Oliver! is a truly British musical, based upon the classic novel Oliver Twist by Charles Dickens.

The show was the first adaptation from a Charles Dickens book to become a stage hit. A Christmas Carol had previously been adapted in the 1950s for television but it was Oliver! that made history when it opened on London's West End in 1960.

The music and lyrics for Oliver! were written by Lionel Bart. Interestingly, when facing severe financial difficulties, he sold the rights for Oliver! to Max Bygraves for £350. When Oliver! became a huge hit, Bygraves sold the rights for £250,000.

The show opened on the West End at the New Theatre, now the Noel Coward Theatre, and ran for 2618 performances. Peter Coe was the director, the choreographer being Malcolm Clare.

There was stiff competition in the original casting: famously, Michael Caine stated he cried for a week after failing to secure the part of Sykes!

The story of Oliver! is set in Victorian England. The name Oliver Twist is given to a boy born in the workhouse orphanage, his mother dying in childbirth. Oliver manages to escape the workhouse and also his harsh work placements and makes his way for London.

He is welcomed into a group of other young boys by the Artful Dodger. Oliver is initially unaware that these boys are really a band of pickpockets run by Fagin. An associate of Fagin, Bill Sykes who has a girlfriend called Nancy , devoted to him despite his abuse of her, looks after Oliver when he discovers what Fagin and the boys actually do.

When Oliver comes to the attention of

wealthy Mr Brownlow, Bill sees Oliver both as an asset and liability. Nancy has to decide whether to be loyal to Bill or do what is best for Oliver. She helps him escape, knowing that Brownlow is looking for Oliver when he learns of his true heritage.

After closing in London, Oliver! transferred to America. It was previewed in Los Angeles using the sets from London that had been shipped by sea. The show opened on Broadway at the Imperial Theatre in 1963 and ran for 774 performances. The production was a critical success and received 10 Tony Award nominations, winning Best Original Score, Best Conductor and Musical Director and Best Scenic Design.

In 1968, Oliver was adapted for film. The original Fagin, Ron Moody was cast along with Jack Wilde, Oliver Reed, Mark Lester, Harry Secombe and Leonard Rossiter. The film was a huge success, winning six Academy Awards including Best Picture.

Oliver! has successfully been revived many times. In 1994, Cameron Macintosh produced a lavish show which opened at the London Palladium, included in the production team at the time was a young Sam Mendes as director, Anthony Ward as designer and Matthew Bourne as choreographer.

The show went on to be revived again in 2009, starring Rowan Atkinson playing Fagin. When Atkinson fell ill, Russ Abbott replaced him, The role then being taken over by Griff Rhys Jones in December of the same year.

Oliver has successfully toured in Australia, America and England. It has also been produced worldwide and continues to enjoy success in its many productions.

In 2013, Cameron Mackintosh announced that a remake of Oliver May take place with a release date aimed for 2016.

Porgy and Bess

It was George Gershwin in 1935 who conceived the idea of producing Porgy and Bess as an American folk opera, the entire cast to be classically trained African American singers.

Although it was first performed in 1935, the work was not widely accepted in America as a legitimate opera until 1976. The show has not been without its problems, as some critics have considered Porgy and Bess to be a racist portrayal of African Americans.

The story, based on DuBose Heyward's novel Porgy which he co-wrote with his wife Dorothy, centres around the romance between Bess, an itinerant woman and Porgy a crippled beggar. Bess belongs to Crown, a powerful and short tempered stevedore. In a drunken rage, Crown commits murder over a game of dice and flees, leaving Bess to fend for herself. She is refused shelter by the other residents of Catfish Row but is welcomed by Porgy into his hovel. An unlikely romance blossoms and Porgy's life begins to change for the better.

Eventually Bess is accepted into Catfish Row and is invited to a picnic on a nearby island. Porgy stays behind and left unprotected, Bess is found by Crown who forces her to submit to him. Bess suffers from a mysterious fever but on her recovery, confesses to Porgy that she has been with Crown, she begs Porgy to protect her when Crown returns.

He duly does, and against the odds murders Crown. Whilst Porgy is in prison, Bess is lured away to New York. On his release from prison, Porgy learns Bess has left and he makes the decision to go to New York to find her, the opera closing with Porgy beginning his long journey.

The opera has been reproduced and revived many times, most notably by Trevor Nunn at the Savoy Theatre in 2006. He had first produced the new adaptation at the Glyndebourne Festival in 1986, the work being highly acclaimed.

The musical was then renamed the Gershwin's Porgy and Bess, Nunn using the dialogue from the original novel and subsequent Broadway stage play. In this production, he did not use operatic voices but relied on his actors. Although the musical garnered mostly positive reviews, the production closed early due to poor box office numbers.

In 2011, the production opened on Broadway and was nominated for 10 Tony Awards, winning Best Revival of a Musical and Best Performance of the Leading Actress in a Musical for Audra McDonald.

Porgy and Bess has had many adaptations for television, film and radio. In 1958, Miles Davis and Gil Evans recorded jazz arrangements from the opera, which was highly successful and was re-released in 1997. Many songs from Porgy and Bess such as "Summertime" and "It Ain't Necessarily So" have become popular in their own right and

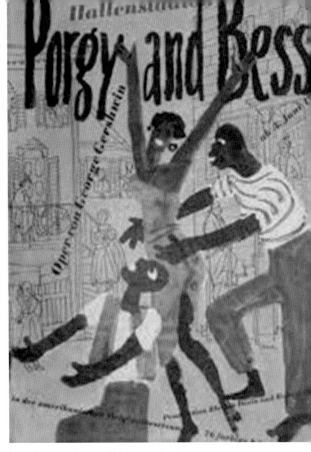

have become jazz and blues standards.

The most recent revival of the Gershwin's Porgy and Bess won the 2012 Tony Award for Best Revival of the Musical and is currently touring America.

Salad Days

Salad Days has been served up successfully around the world since it first appeared on the menu at the Theatre Royal, Bristol, some 60 years ago.

The musical's enduring popularity lies in its light-hearted innocence and apparent simplicity, in sharp contrast to the myriad "hard-nosed" American musicals of the era, and its bright score including the songs "We Said We Wouldn't Look Back", "I Sit in the Sun" and "We're Looking for a Piano".

Julian Slade and Dorothy Reynolds wrote both the music and lyrics. The title is taken from William Shakespeare's Antony and Cleopatra - "My salad days, When I was green in judgment, cold in blood, To say as I said then!" - and the phrase has come to be used generally to refer to one's days of youthful inexperience.

The lightweight plot centre around university sweethearts Jane and Timothy Dawes who meet in a park, soon after their graduation, to plan their lives. They agree to get married, and do so in secret, but Timothy's parents have urged him to ask his various influential relatives—a Minister, a Foreign Office official, a General, a scientist—to find him suitable employment.

He and Jane decide, however, that he must take the first job that he is offered. A passing tramp offers them £7 a week to look after his mobile piano for a month, and, upon accepting, they discover that when the piano plays it gives everyone within earshot an irresistible desire to dance!

After attempts by the Minister of Pleasure and Pastime (Timothy's Ministerial uncle) to ban the disruptive

music, the piano vanishes, and Timothy enlists his scientific Uncle Zed to take them in his flying saucer to retrieve it. When it is found, the tramp reappears to tell them that their month is up and the piano must be passed on to another couple. He also reveals that he is a hitherto unknown uncle of Timothy (whose parents had referred to "the one we don't mention"). Timothy and Jane look forward to the future with confidence.

Salad Days premiered in the UK at the Theatre Royal, Bristol in June 1954, and transferred to the Vaudeville Theatre in London on 5 August 1954, running for 2,283 performances to become the longest-running show in musical theatre history until overtaken by My Fair Lady in the US (1956) and Oliver! in the U.K. (1960). In the Evening Standard Awards for 1955, Salad Days was given the Award for Most Enjoyable Show (although The Pyjama Game won as Best Musical).

The musical was produced by Denis Carey, with dances arranged by Elizabeth West, and with a cast that featured Dorothy Reynolds in a variety of roles, John Warner as Timothy and Eleanor Drew as Jane. Slade played one of the two pianos. The reviewer in The Guardian wrote: "There is no pointed satire, only a passable line of wit, but the effect is one of genuine high spirits and those who liked it on Thursday were ready to call it the gayest piece of entertainment since The Mikado. Others were heard to compare it to a children's party, meaning that they found the fun jejune, 'undergraduate,' and limited."

Nonetheless Salad Days went on to enjoy many revivals, most recently being performed at the Riverside Studios in London in 2009. This run was a sell-out and the production was revived again for Christmas and New Year in 2012–13.

Show Boat

The musical of Show Boat was first produced in 1927. The book and lyrics were by Oscar Hammerstein II with the music by Jerome Kern. It was based on the best selling novel by Edna Ferber.

Show Boat was immediately recognised for its quality and became a watershed moment in the history of American musicals. The production was a radical departure in musical storytelling compared to the trivial and unrealistic operettas from the 1890s Broadway productions.

Awards for Broadway shows did not exist in 1927 when Show Boat was first premiered, nor for the 1932 revival, however more recent revivals for Show Boat have lavished praise on the musical. In 1995, it won the Tony Award for Best Revival of a Musical and the Laurence Olivier Award for Best Musical Revival in 1991.

The story of Show Boat is based at the end of the 19th century and centres around a show boat named Cotton Blossom owned by Hawk family. It tells of its journeys along the rivers in the south of North America where everyone comes for great musical entertainment. Julie Laverne and her husband are stars of the show however, when the local police learn that Julie who is half African American and married to a white man, they are forced to leave the boat as inter-racial marriages are forbidden. Magnolia Hawk now becomes the new show boat attraction with her leading man Gaylord Ravenal who is a gambler. They instantly fall in love and marry, much to the disapproval of Magnolia's family. They leave the boat and soon Magnolia realizes that gambling means more to Gaylord than anything else. He gambles away their fortune and leaves her, not knowing she is pregnant. Magnolia is now forced to fend for herself and make a new start in life.

On first reading the book, Jerome Kern asked to be introduced to author Edna Ferber and expressed his hope of adapting it for a musical. Ferber, at first shocked, then granted him and Oscar Hammerstein the rights to set the novel to music. When they first auditioned their material for producer Florenz Ziegfield, he stated it was the best musical comedy he had ever been fortunate enough to get hold of.

The original production ran for over four hours but was trimmed to be just over three before it got to Broadway. In 1927, Show Boat went on a pre-Broadway tour and then opened at the Ziegfield Theatre in December of the same year to great critical acclaim. The show was a stunning success: it ran for a year and a half and was performed 572 times.

The production then toured extensively and was revived on Broadway at the Casino Theatre in 1932 with most of the original cast. It went on to be revived many times on Broadway, notably starring Mickey Rooney in the 1983 production at the Kennedy Centre in Washington DC.

Show Boat originally opened at the Theatre Royal, Drury Lane in 1928 and

has subsequently been revived many times in the West End including a run of 909 performances at the Adelphi Theatre in 1971.

In 1998, the Hal Prince production at the Prince Edward Theatre was nominated for the Olivier Award of Outstanding Musical Production.

Show Boat has also been adapted for film, radio and television. In 1939, Orson Wells directed and introduced a non-musical version of the story for the Campbell Playhouse.

The show has not been without controversy, primarily for the use of the racially-charged "n" word in the lyrics. Many subsequent productions have changed the lyrics, but many believe that Kern and Hammerstein used the word in an ironic way to give a sympathetic voice to an oppressed people.

Show Boat will long remain in the history of musicals as one of the most innovative of its time.

Singin' In the Rain

While many musical films are based on the stage originals, Singin' in the Rain is a rare example of the reverse, starting life as a blockbuster film and was then later adapted for the stage.

The musical originated from a book written by Betty Comden and Adolph Green, the lyrics for the production were by Arthur Freed and the music written by Nacio Herb Brown.

The film was released in 1952, and immediately became an overnight hit, wowing audiences all over the world. It continues to be on the list of many movie critics' favourite films. Star of the show, Gene Kelly also directed the film which featured songs written by both Nacio Herb Brown and Arthur Reed.

The musical of Singin' in the Rain had to make several changes from the film version, including the montage of stunts on set such as jumping off the top of a bus into the car. However, fans of the film were treated to all the favourite songs as well as a few that were not.

The original screenplay by Comden and Green is fairly true to the original dialogue as both did the adaptation for the theatre. The director and choreographer for the musical, Cheryl Sonchey used most of the original choreography produced by Gene Kelly and Stanley Donen and adapted it seemlessly for the stage.

The story follows silent film star, Don Lockwood, a musician, dancer and stuntman. His leading lady, Lina Lamont is barely tolerated by him, however she is convinced that their screen romance is real. Their first talking picture becomes a smash hit so head of the studio, R. F. Simpson decides he will convert their

new film into a talky. The production goes badly, Lina Lamont's voice being appalling. Cosmo Brown, Don's best friend decide that they should dub Gina's voice and turn the film into a musical comedy. Don falls in love with the young Kathy Seldon who is providing the voice for Lena. Lena discovers the affair and does everything possible to sabotage their romance. After a tremendously successful premiere, the audience clamour for Lina to sing and whilst she begins to sing, believing she will be lip synced, the curtain is raised behind her revealing her deception and Kathy singing. Kathy becomes a star and Lina is finished.

The musical opened at the London Palladium in London's West End in 1983 and ran until September 1985. It was directed by Tommy Steele with choreographer being Peter Gennaro. The production was nominated for a Laurence Olivier Award in Best Actress in a Musical category for Sarah Payne.

Singin' in the Rain then opened on Broadway at the Gershwin Theatre, directed and choreographed by Twyla Tharp. The show ran for 367 performances with 38 previews. It was nominated for two Tony Awards, Best Book of a Musical and Best Performance by Leading Actor in a Musical.

The show enjoyed an extensive successful tour of the United Kingdom in 1994 again being directed by Tommy Steele and starring Paul Nicholas as Don. A successful revival was staged at the Olivier Theatre in 2000, and went on to be revived at the Sadler's Wells Theatre in 2004.

Singin' in the Rain recently enjoyed a successful tour of the UK , having been revived at the Chichester Festival Theatre in 2011. This adaptation transferred to the Palace Theatre in the West End and has been a slickly orchestrated operation, especially with the execution of the title song "Singin' in the Rain" as the show requires 7000 litres of water each time it rains on stage, 2500 litres falling from above and 4500 litres splashing from below. As it rains twice during each performance a total of 14,000 litres of water are used during each performance.

South Pacific

It is fair to say that South Pacific, composed by Rodgers and Hammerstein, is one of the most famous American musicals of all time. It opened to rave reviews and is considered a classic in its confrontation of racism.

The original work was based on the 1947 Pulitzer Prize winning book "Tales of the South Pacific" written by James A Michener. Both Rogers and Hammerstein had already become successful with massive hits such as Oklahoma! and Carousel, and agreed to work on South Pacific as they believed it would be financially successful as well as sending a strong progressive message on racism.

The story is based around an American nurse stationed on an island in the South Pacific during World War II. She falls in love with a middle aged French plantation owner but is struggling to accept his mixed race children.

While another romance, between a young Tonkinese woman and an American lieutenant, is put in jeopardy as he fears for the social consequences of a marriage to his Asian sweetheart.

In 1949, South Pacific opened at the Majestic Theatre on Broadway. The advance sale for tickets was $400,000 with an additional $700,000 being made in sales soon after the opening night.

Indeed, the opening night was frequently stopped after the audience broke out into spontaneous applause which was sustained at length when the final curtain was called.

The show received rave reviews and won four Tony Awards including Best Musical, Best Score and Best Libretto. It is the only musical production in history to win in all four acting categories. It finally closed in January 1954 after running for 1925 performances. The only cast member remaining from the original performance, Myron McCormick, led the audience in a final rendition of "Auld Lang Syne,": the curtain did not fall but remained raised as the audience left the theatre.

In 1951, South Pacific opened at the Theatre Royal, Drury Lane in London's West End. The show continued to be a sensational success, running for more than 800 performances.

The most memorable songs from the show include "Some Enchanted Evening", "I'm Gonna Wash That Man Right Outa My Hair" and "Happy Talk."

The musical was made into a film in 1958 and immediately became a box office hit. It was directed by Joshua Logan and won the Academy Award for Best Sound. It was also nominated for the Best Scoring of a Musical Picture.

South Pacific has continued to be successfully produced around the world, most notably in London in 2008 when the show won seven Tony Awards, including Best Revival, and five Drama Desk Awards including Outstanding Musical Review. The most recent London production in 2011 received three

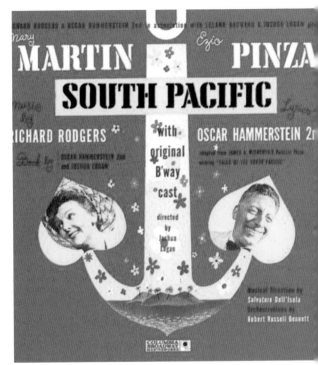

Olivier Award nominations including Best Musical Revival.

South Pacific will continue to mesmerize audiences with its superb songs but will also be remembered for the huge cultural impact it had in tackling the prickly subject of racism so successfully.

Spamalot

Spamalot is a musical comedy which originated from the 1975 film Monty Python and the Holy Grail with its creator one of the original Pythons, Eric Idle.

Although Idle wrote the spin-off book and lyrics, he collaborated with John Du Prez for some of the music.

The songs "Knights of the Round Table" and "Brave Sir Robin" were composed by Neil Innes, originally for the Monty Python and the Holy Grail film. The other memorable song included in the musical is "Always Look on the Bright Side of Life," which was written by Idle for the film Monty Python's Life of Brian.

The title of the musical was first tested on US audiences, who loved it, and comes from a line in the film "we eat ham, and jam and Spam a lot."

The story of Spamalot runs on the same track as the Python's Holy Grail, following King Arthur and his squire Patsy with a selection of knights on their quest to find the holy grail. The quest leads them to a French castle and into the dangerous clutches of the Black Knight and extremely dangerous killer rabbit. Unlike the film, however, Spamalot is "all singing and all dancing silliness."

The show was previewed at the Shubert Theatre in Chicago in December 2004 going on to open at the New York Shubert Theatre on Broadway in February 2005. Immediately popular with both critics and audiences, the production was nominated for 14 Tony Awards, winning the Award for Best Musical.

Under the direction of Mike Nichols, the show played for 1,575 performances, closing in January 2009 after entertaining more than two million people and grossing $175 million. The production recouped its initial production costs in less than six months.

The original cast members on the Broadway performance included Tim Curry as King Arthur and a recording of Jonathan Cleese, one of the original Python stars, as the voice of God.

The show went on to tour America twice, initially in Spring 2006, going on to win three touring Broadway Awards in 2007. Spamalot returned to Chicago, with Richard Chamberlain taking over as King Arthur and then toured again in the summer of 2009.

In London, Spamalot opened at the Palace Theatre on Shaftesbury Avenue in 2006 to rave reviews and tickets for the show were booked up until November 2008. Tim Curry returned to the production for the opening run, while other famous actors taking part have included Alan Dale, Peter Davison and Bill Ward.

The show received seven nominations in the 2007 Laurence Olivier Awards ceremony. After the London production closed in 2009, there have been several revivals, one including various celebrities playing the role of God for charity: these

included Gary Lineker, Barbara Windsor, Brian May and Michael Palin.

The show is currently on tour in the UK with Phil Jupitus starring as King Arthur. Spamalot has been produced throughout the world, notably in Australia and New Zealand where the Python humour is much revered and appreciated.

Starlight Express

Starlight Express is one of the longest running musicals ever to be produced in the West End.

It is a rock musical with all the actors famously performing whilst wearing rollerskates. The music was written by Andrew Lloyd Webber with lyrics by Richard Stilgoe. Television dance trouper Arlene Phillips was the main choreographer.

Lloyd Webber had originally planned to adapt the musical from the children's books of Rev W Awdrey featuring Thomas the Tank Engine. However, when Audrey wouldn't allow Lloyd Webber permission to use the characters in the way he wished, he changed tack, and story became more like that of Cinderella.

The music in Starlight Express is similar to the style of Joseph and the Amazing Technicolor Dreamcoat with great dollops of disco and 1980s pop rock and the occasional pastiche of blues rap country and gospel music.

Starlight Express is also similar to Lloyds Webber's vision of Cats, in that it uses its actors to portray inanimate characters, this time trains not felines. The actors, wearing elaborate costumes, recreate the effect of trains on tracks by riding around the theatre on roller skates. The plot is the story of the characters involved in the race and the songs from Starlight Express are much more a collection of individual songs rather than a direct link to the storyline.

The cast for Starlight Express were trained for several months in rollerskating techniques before their performances, however the demands of the show often lead to accidents and injuries.

Starlight Express, produced by Trevor Nunn, opened at the Apollo Victoria Theatre in the West End with one of the most spectacular stage sets ever created. The set included a six ton steel bridge which lifted and tilted to connect with various levels of the set during the races, a steeply banked central area and sweeping racetracks that extended into and around the auditorium, allowing the actors to race on the track from the stalls and end up in the dress circle.

The musical then moved on to Broadway, opening at the Gershwin Theatre in 1987 and running for 761 performances. Sadly, this production was not able to extend into the auditorium as it did in London, so instead, the race tracks were spiralled up and around the theatre. The set was far more decorated than that of its London counterpart and included American place names and scenes from the country to give a sense of location to each part of the track.

The name Starlight Express was taken from the 1950s to early 60s Glasgow to London Service, which only ran at weekends and holidays and was offered at cheaper prices using special routing and unusual locomotives.

Starlight Express was light years ahead

of its time, a futuristic tale of love and hope in the face of adversity which fused state of the art technology with dazzling sets and choreography.

Summer Holiday

Summer Holiday was a spin-off of the famous British musical film of the early 1960s starring Cliff Richard.

It was only in the mid 1990s that it was adapted for the stage. The show premiered at the Opera House in Blackpool in 1996 with Darren Day playing Cliff's romantic lead role and then went on a national tour before returning to Blackpool in 1998.

The story of a Summer Holiday is set in 1963, the year that Beatlemania was born and the Profumo affair scandalised Britain. It follows four mechanics from a London bus depot who decided to refurbish a double-decker and use it as a hotel whilst driving around Europe, their intention being to set up a whole fleet.

Whilst driving in France, they pick up three girls whose car has broken down and agree to take them to their next job in Athens. On the way, they also pick up a stowaway who is a young American boy.

In the news meanwhile, a young American female singer has gone missing and her ambitious mother feeds the story to the press to get as much publicity as possible.

Eventually, the young American boy is discovered to be the missing young American girl singer. The main character, played by Cliff Richard in the film, falls in love with her. When they reach Athens however, the mechanics are arrested for kidnapping, but in front of her mother and a room filled with the world press, Barbara and Don declare their love for each other. Ahh!

The stage musical differed in a number of respects from the film version. For example, the route to Athens is via Italy rather than the original film route via

Yugoslavia. The songs also differ, and include a number of songs from Cliff Richard's other early back catalogue, such as "The Young Ones."

Many of the songs from the film and musical reached the higher echelons of the British charts including "Summer Holiday," " The Next Time," "Bachelor Boy" and "Foot Tapper."

In 2003, Summer Holiday packed its bags for another nationwide UK tour starring Stefan Booth; and then later in the run, Darren Day reprising his earlier headlining role.

The Bodyguard

That the Hollywood movie The Bodyguard had been such a worldwide smash, it was arguably only a matter of time before its success would be repeated on the stage.

The original film was made in 1992 and starred Whitney Houston, many of whose songs were also featured in the movie, alongside Kevin Costner as her bodyguard.

It became the second highest grossing film worldwide that year, taking $411 million, and its spin-off album became the best selling soundtrack of all time.

The Bodyguard was written as a book by Alexander Dinelaris while Lawrence Kasdan adapted the film's original screenplay including some more of Whitney Houston's other hits such as "Saving All My Love For You," "So Emotional," "I Wanna Dance With

Somebody" and "How Will I Know".

The story of The Bodyguard opens with a pop singer who has been receiving threatening notes and in consequence of this, her manager hires a bodyguard for her. The singer is not initially impressed with him and is annoyed by the tightening security that she and her entourage feel is more than is necessary. Eventually, the bodyguard and singer start an affair and she finally begins to believe his precautions are necessary when a stalker strikes close to home.

Alexander Dinelaris had brought the story forward to present day, with the lead character of Rachel Marron featuring more heavily than that of the bodyguard.

Following the tragic death of Whitney Houston, star of the stage show Heather Headley debated whether to pull out of the role of Rachel as she feared being

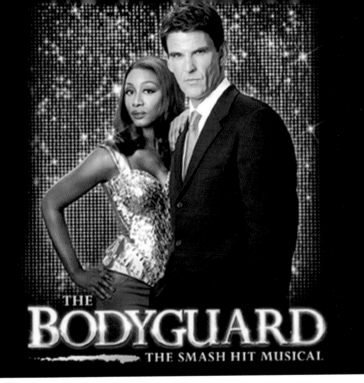

THE BODYGUARD

THE SMASH HIT MUSICAL

unfavourably compared to the late star. However she decided to carry on, trying to make the songs her own but acknowledging and keeping the integrity of Whitney Houston's music.

The Bodyguard premiered at the Adelphi Theatre in London's West End in 2012, and took advanced sales of more than £4 million. Subsequently its booking at the Adelphi was extended until September 2014.

Several future productions are planned for The Bodyguard, its producer David Ian looking at Broadway in America, Australia, Germany and the Far East.

The biggest song of The Bodyguard is Dolly Parton's composition "I Will Always Love You" – which it seems is exactly how audiences feel about this slick show.

The Boy Friend

The Boy Friend was successful both on the West End and on Broadway. The musical was written by Sandy Wilson and follows in the style of the comic pastiches of 1920s shows, especially those of the Rodgers and Hart musicals such as The Girl Friend.

The story of The Boy Friend begins in Madam Dubonnet's finishing school on the French Riviera and follows the lives of five young British girls who are planning to attend a ball that evening. One of the girls called Polly falls in love with Tony, a delivery boy. Taking advice from her father who had warned her to be aware of boys dating her for money, Polly pretends to be a secretary.

When Polly's parents arrive in Nice with Lord and Lady Brockhurst, things get complicated, as it turns out that the Brockhursts are really Tony's wealthy parents. Polly and Tony have been sharing the same secret and when the cat is let out of the bag, all ends well.

The show ran for 2078 performances in London making it the third longest running musical in 1954 before it was surpassed by Salad Days. The Boy Friend initially opened at the Players Theatre Club in 1953; then transferring to the Embassy Theatre in Swiss Cottage; and in 1954, moved again to the Wyndham Theatre in London's West End. The Boy Friend immediately proved immensely popular with the British public and continued to run in the West End for more than five years.

The Boy Friend then opened on Broadway at the Royale Theatre in 1954 and starred newcomer Julie Andrews who was acting in her Broadway debut as Polly. The show ran for one year and closed after 485 performances. Julie

Andrews received the Theatre World Award for her performance and was soon catapulted to fame playing Eliza Dolittle in My Fair Lady after its producers had seen her performance in The Boy Friend.

The show has become popular for many revivals by both professional and amateur ensembles as the cast is relatively small and production costs are low.

In 2003, The Boy Friend was produced at the Bay Street Theatre in New York with Julie Andrews making her directorial debut. The show moved to the Goodspeed Opera house in 2005 and then continued to tour the United States playing in 11 cities.

Ken Russell produced a film version of The Boy Friend in 1971, weaving the basic plot into a more complicated story with a seaside dramatic company performing the show which is then visited by a film producer.

The film starred Twiggy and Glenda Jackson. The National Board of Review voted Ken Russell Best Director and at the Golden Globe Awards, Twiggy won both Best Newcomer and Best Actress (for a musical/comedy.) When the film opened in America however, it did not fair well, perhaps due to the fact that MGM had edited it down by nearly half an hour to 109 minutes.

The King and I

The history of The King and I is inexorably linked with charismatic bald actor Yul Bryner.

He not only starred in the stage show but reprised his role as the King on the big screen for which he won an Oscar as Best Actor.

The King and I was the fifth musical written by the now famous team of Rogers and Hammerstein. The show was based upon the 1944 book by Margaret Landon called Anna and the King of Siam.

When British actress Gertrude Lawrence's business manager and theatrical attorney Fanny Holtzman was sent the novel by Landon, she approached Cole Porter to write the score, however he declined. Fanny had decided to then ask Noel Coward, but on meeting Oscar Hammerstein's wife Dorothy, she then approached both Rogers and Hammerstein and asked them to turn the book into a musical. The pair were both initially reluctant but agreed to produce the musical.

The King and I was a huge success, it ran for 1246 performances on Broadway and there followed a hit London run and US national tour.

The story begins in Siam in 1862, when English widow Anna and her young son arrive at the Royal Palace in Bangkok having been summoned by the king to serve as a tutor for his many children and wives. Although the King is considered to be a barbarian by those in the West, he asks Anna to help in changing his image. Whilst keeping a firm grip on their respective traditions and values, Anna and the King begin to understand and come to respect one another in a bizarre love story.

The show first opened on Broadway in 1951, both the press and public expected it to become a huge hit, however both Hammerstein and Rogers were said to be concerned that the show was not as good as South Pacific.

Yul Brynner, in the role of the king almost stole the show, but leading lady Gertrude Lawrence also put in a dazzling performance. Tragically Lawrence was not to know she was dying from liver cancer: she became ill during her performances and eventually in 1952 fainted following a matinee. She slipped into a coma and died that September. She was buried in one of the ball gowns from the show and the lights of both Broadway and the West End were dimmed for her funeral.

The King and I won numerous awards including a Tony Award for Gertrude Lawrence whilst Yul Brynner won the award for Best Featured Actor, the show also won the Tony for Best Musical.

In London, the production opened in 1953 at the Theatre Royal, Drury Lane, the production was warmly received by both audiences and critics alike, running for 946 performances,

In 1956, The King and I was adapted for film. Yul Brynner played opposite

Deborah Kerr with the film being directed by Walter Lange. It was a huge hit, winning five Academy Awards and being nominated for four more. Brynner won an Oscar as Best Actor and Kerr was nominated as Best Actress. However, it should be noted that the Thai officials judged the film to be offensive to their monarchy and banned both the film and musical from their country.

The King and I has gone to gone on to have many revivals internationally and has featured in many of the world's best theatres. The musical remains a popular choice for local community theatres, school, university groups and regional theatre companies.

The Lion King

The stage version of The Lion King is one of a select few musicals that was based on a blockbuster children's film rather than the other way around.

The original Walt Disney film, produced in 1994, featured a large vocal cast and included actors such as Matthew Broderick, Jeremy Irons, James Earl Jones and Moira Kelly. The film was praised by the critics and grossed over $987 million. It won two Academy Awards and the Golden Globe award for Best Motion Picture.

The lyricist was Tim Rice, who having been invited to write the songs for the film, only accepted on the condition that he found his own composing partner. He suggested Elton John after Benny Andersson from Abba turned it down.

The pair wrote five original songs for the film, with Elton John singing "Can You Feel The Love Tonight?" at the end of the movie. The original motion picture soundtrack was the fourth bestselling album of the year and the top selling soundtrack.

The sentimental story is pure Disney. Simba, a young lion prince, born into the royal family, spends most of his days exploring the Savannah and idolising his kingly father Mufasa. When tragedy strikes and his father is killed, orchestrated by Simba's wicked uncle Scar, Simba flees, leaving the life he knew behind. He is befriended by two hilarious and unlikely friends and Simba's life starts anew. He receives a desperate plea to return to the tribe and Simba must now take on a formidable enemy and fulfil his destiny to be king.

The Lion King was first produced on stage at the Orpheum Theatre,

Minneapolis, Minnesota. It became an instant success and went on to premiere on Broadway in 1997 at the New Amsterdam Theatre. In 2006, the show moved to the Minskoff Theatre and is still running there, having been performed over 6700 times. The Lion King is now the fourth longest running show on Broadway history and has grossed more than $1 billion, making it the most financially successful Broadway production of all time. The show received eleven nominations for the Drama Desk Awards, winning eight of them. It was also nominated for eleven Tony Awards and won five of them in 1998.

In 1999, The Lion King opened at the Lyceum Theatre on London's West End and is still running to this day. The show was nominated for three Laurence Olivier awards and won Best Theatre Choreographer and Best Costume Design. In 2008 the cast of The Lion King were asked to perform at the Royal Variety Performance, held at the London Palladium in the presence of the British Royal family, which they did to huge applause.

The production of the Lion King has now been seen by over 70 million people around the world and is still wowing audiences in London, New York, Tokyo, Hamburg, Madrid, São Paulo and Sydney.

The Phantom
of the Opera

The Phantom of the Opera is arguably Andrew Lloyd Webber's greatest triumph.

Based on the French novel Le Fantôme de l'Opéra by Gaston Leroux, the central plot revolves around a beautiful soprano, Christine Daaé, who becomes the obsession of a mysterious, disfigured musical genius.

The musical opened in London's West End in 1986, and on Broadway in 1988 and has gone on to smash box office records ever since.

It won the 1986 Olivier Award and the 1988 Tony Award for Best Musical, and Michael Crawford (in the title role) won the Olivier and Tony Awards for Best Actor in a Musical. It is the longest running show in Broadway history by a wide margin, and celebrated its 10,000th Broadway performance on the 11th of February 2012, the first production ever to do so. It is the second longest-running West End musical, and the third longest-running West End show overall.

In 1984, Lloyd Webber contacted Cameron Mackintosh, the co-producer of Cats and Song and Dance, to create a new romantic musical based on Gaston Leroux's book The Phantom of the Opera. They screened both the 1925 Lon Chaney and the 1943 Claude Rains motion picture versions, but neither saw an effective way to make the leap from film to stage.

Later, in New York, Lloyd Webber found a second-hand copy of the original, long-out-of-print Leroux novel, which supplied the necessary inspiration to develop a musical.

Lloyd Webber first approached Jim Steinman to write the lyrics, but he declined in order to fulfill his commitments on a Bonnie Tyler album. Alan Jay Lerner was then recruited, but he became seriously ill after joining the project and was forced to withdraw; none of his contributions (mostly involving the song "Masquerade") are credited in the show.

Richard Stilgoe, the lyricist for Starlight Express, wrote most of the original lyrics for the production. Charles Hart, a young and then-relatively unknown lyricist, later rewrote many of the lyrics, along with original lyrics for "Think of Me". Some of Stilgoe's original contributions are still present in the final version.

Inspired in part by an earlier musical version of the same story by Ken Hill, Lloyd Webber's score is sometimes operatic in style but maintains the form and structure of a musical throughout. The full-fledged operatic passages are reserved principally for subsidiary characters such as Andre and Firmin, Carlotta, and Piangi.

Maria Björnson designed the sets and over 200 costumes, including the elaborate gowns in the "Masquerade" sequence. Her set designs, including the chandelier, subterranean gondola, and sweeping staircase, earned her multiple awards. Hal Prince, director of Cabaret,

Candide, Follies, and Lloyd Webber's Evita, directed the production, while Gillian Lynne, associate director and choreographer of Cats, provided the integral musical staging and choreography.

A preview of the first act was staged at Sydmonton (Lloyd Webber's home) in 1985, starring Colm Wilkinson (later the star of the Toronto production) as the Phantom, Sarah Brightman as Kristin (later Christine) and Clive Carter (later a member of the London cast) as Raoul. This very preliminary production used Stilgoe's original unaltered lyrics, and many songs sported names that were later changed, such as "What Has Time Done to Me" ("Think of Me"), and "Papers" ("Notes"). The Phantom's original mask covered the entire face and remained in place throughout the performance, obscuring the actor's vision and muffling his voice. Björnson designed the now-iconic half-mask to replace it, and the unmasking sequence was added. Clips of this preview performance were included on the DVD of the 2004 film production.

Phantom began previews at Her Majesty's Theatre in London's West End on the 27th September 1986 under the direction of Hal Prince, then opened on the 9th October.

It was choreographed by Gillian Lynne and the sets were designed by Maria Björnson, with lighting by Andrew Bridge. Michael Crawford starred in the title role with Sarah Brightman as Christine and Steve Barton as Raoul. The production, still playing at Her Majesty's, celebrated its 10,000th performance on the 23rd of October 2010, with Lloyd Webber and the original Phantom, Michael Crawford, in attendance. It is the second longest-running musical in West End (and world) history behind Les Misérables.

A 25th-anniversary stage performance was held in London on the 1st and 2nd of October 2011 at the Royal Albert Hall and was screened live in cinemas worldwide.

The production was produced by Cameron Mackintosh, directed by Laurence Connor, musical staging & choreography by Gillian Lynne, set design by Matt Kinley, costume design by Maria Björnson, lighting design by Patrick Woodroffe and sound design by Mick Potter. The cast included Ramin Karimloo as the Phantom, Sierra Boggess as Christine, Hadley Fraser as Raoul, Wynne Evans as Piangi, Wendy Ferguson as Carlotta, Barry James as Monsieur Firmin, Gareth Snook as Monsieur Andre, Liz Robertson as Madame Giry and Daisy Maywood as Meg Giry. Lloyd Webber and several original cast members, including Crawford and Brightman, were in attendance.

In March 2012 a new production directed by Laurence Connor began a UK and Ireland tour to commemorate the 25th anniversary of the show, beginning at the Theatre Royal Plymouth and traveling to Manchester, Bristol, Dublin, Leeds, Edinburgh, Milton Keynes, Cardiff and Southampton. John Owen-Jones and Earl Carpenter alternated as the Phantom with Katie Hall as Christine and Simon Bailey as Raoul.

Phantom began Broadway previews at the Majestic Theatre on the 9th January 1988 and opened on the 26th of January. Crawford, Brightman, and Barton took their respective roles from the West End. The production continues to play at the Majestic, where it became the first Broadway musical in history to surpass 10,000 performances on the 11th February 2012. On the 26th January 2013 the production celebrated its 25th anniversary with its 10,400th performance. It is, by more than 3,000 performances, the longest-running show in Broadway history.

The Rocky Horror Picture Show

The Rocky Horror Picture Show was the brainchild of actor, writer and television presenter Richard O'Brien.

He wrote the book, music and lyrics whilst out of work through the winter of 1973, combining his passion for science fiction and B horror movies.

Jim Sharman, a director friend to O'Brien, helped him finish the title and asked to direct it. The first viewing took place at the Royal Court Theatre in Sloane Square, Chelsea but only as an experimental project.

The long-time star of the show Tim Curry first became aware of the musical after a chance meeting with O'Brien outside an old gym in Paddington Street, London. After his first reading of the script, he knew it would go on to be a smash hit.

Michael White was brought in to produce the show and it premiered without an interval at the Royal Court's Upstairs Theatre in 1973. The show was a critical and commercial success and transferred to the Chelsea Classic Cinema in August and then found a home in the Kings Road Theatre in November, which could seat 500 people.

Record producer Jonathan King had seen the show on its second night and immediately signed up the cast to make a recording and became heavily involved in its initial promotion.

The Rocky Horror Picture Show went on to win the Evening Standard Award for Best Musical and ran for nearly 3000 performances before closing in September 1980.

The musical tells strange story of a young engaged couple, they get caught in a storm and try to find sanctuary in

the home of a mad transvestite scientist who unveils his new muscle man creation named Rocky Horror.

In 1975, the musical was adapted for film, again directed by Sharman and starring Tim Curry, Susan Sarandon and Barry Bostwick alongside several more of the original cast. The movie has become a cult classic with late-night audiences dressing up as characters from the film and reciting the lines.

The Rocky Horror Picture Show has been hugely successful in both its revivals and tours. It has recently enjoyed a popular revival of the UK which has now moved to Australia.

The Sound of Music

The tills have been alive with The Sound of Music ever since it was first made into a musical and became one of the highest-grossing films of all time.

Inspired by a memoir written by Maria von Trapp, it was originally made into a film called the "The Trapp Family" which was one of the most successful German films of the 1950s.

On viewing the film, stage director Vincent J Donahue suggested that the picture could be made into a play but soon realised that it would be so much better if it featured songs to compliment the narrative.

Richard Rodgers and Oscar Hammerstein were approached to write the music and lyrics and in 1959, The Sound of Music opened at the Lunt-Fontanne Theatre on Broadway. It moved to the Mark Hellinger Theatre in 1962 and closed in 1963 after 1443 performances.

The show was hugely successful and interestingly tied with Fiorello! for the title of the Best Musical at the Tony Awards. Mary Martin, at the age of 46, was also nominated for Best Actress in a Musical while the entire child cast in the performance were nominated for Best Featured Actress as one single nomination, even though two of the children were boys!

The story of The Sound of Music is set in 1930s Austria and follows a young woman named Maria who abandons her ambition of becoming a nun to take the job as a governess for a navy Captain, Baron George von Trapp, a widower with seven children. Upon her arrival, Maria finds the children unhappy and resentful of the governesses they have had before.

Maria's kindness and understanding soon draws the children to her and she brings some much needed joy into all their lives, Maria and the captain eventually fall in love but their personal lives become overshadowed by world events as Austria is about to come under German control.

In 1961, The Sound of Music premiered at the Palace Theatre in London's West End and went on to run for 2385 performances. Directed by Jerome Whyte, the show featured the original New York choreography, supervised by Joe Layton, and the original sets designed by Oliver Smith.

In 1965, The Sound of Music was made into a star-studded film, directed and produced by Robert Wise with the lead roles taken by Julie Andrews and Christopher Plummer. The film reputedly saved 20th Century Fox from bankruptcy after it had been hit by extremely high production costs and huge financial losses incurred by Cleopatra. On its release, The Sound of Music became the highest grossing film of all time and is the most successful musical movie ever made. It is believed to have ultimately grossed $286 million internationally.

The musical has been revived many times both on Broadway, London and

around the world. Most notably, a 2006 production by Andrew Lloyd Webber ran for more than two years.

Latterly it was also revived at the Open Air Theatre in Regents Park in 2013, becoming the highest grossing production ever at that theatre. The Sound of Music is currently playing at the London Palladium in the West End.

The Wizard of Oz

Theatregoes have been off to see The Wizard of Oz for more than 100 years – laying claim that it is one of the oldest musicals still to be seen on Broadway and in the West End.

The Wizard of Oz was written by L. Frank Baum in 1900 who also adapted it in to a musical although the famous characters of the Wicked Witch and Toto the dog were not in his original musical extravaganza.

The show was premiered in Chicago in 1902 and became a success on Broadway in the following year, continuing to tour for nine years throughout the US.

In 1939, the film of the Wizard of Oz was released and initially failed to recoup the studio's investment and was a relative box office flop. However, interest in it was soon fuelled when it was nominated for six Academy Awards, losing Best Picture to Gone With The Wind, but winning the Best Original Song for "Somewhere Over The Rainbow."

The Wizard of Oz has been subject for many musical theatre adaptations, including one made by the Royal Shakespeare Company in 1987 which closely followed the film version.

After three decades of being apart, Tim Rice and Andrew Lloyd Webber decided to collaborate once more in the production of the Wizard of Oz – Lloyd Webber's 18th musical. The new musical was directed by Jeremy Sams and included several new songs written by Rice and Webber and was adapted from the original 1939 film screenplay.

The Wizard of Oz opened at the London Palladium Theatre on London's West End in March 2011, the title role of the Wizard being played by Michael Crawford and the role of Dorothy by Danielle Hope, who had

been selected through the reality television show "Over the Rainbow".

Several different actors have been brought into play the main character of the Wizard, including Russell Grant and Des O'Connor. The show celebrated 500 performances in May 2012 and closed in September of the same year. It had taken in preopening sales of £10 million. Although the production opened with mixed reviews, it was nominated for the Best Musical Revival in the Laurence Olivier Awards and won two nominations for Best Musical Revival and Best Supporting Actress in a Musical in the Whatson stage.com Theatre Goers Choice Awards.

The Lloyd Webber production of the Wizard of Oz is currently touring throughout the US. There is no doubt that audiences will be following the Yellow Brick Road for many more years to come.

Urinetown

Some may say that the title to this musical stinks, or is taking the proverbial, but few would argue that against the odds it has been awash with awards.

Springing from a book written by Greg Kotis, the show is a satire of the legal system, capitalism and bureaucratic municipal politics in a resonating tale of greed, corruption, love and revolution in a time where water is worth it's weight in gold.

The original idea for Urinetown originated whilst Kotis was travelling for a year in Europe as a student on a budget and his encounters with a pay per use toilet. He began writing the book upon his return and approached Mark Hollman to explore the possibility of producing it as a Broadway show.

Unsurprisingly, there was little interest from production companies, but an experimental theatre group called the Neo Futurists based in Chicago decided to produce Urinetown in 1999. When these plans fell through, it was the New York fringe festival producer John Clancy that decided to step in. On seeing the show for the first time, playwright David Auburn, a personal friend of both Kotis and Hollman immediately made a call to the production company the Araca group who commissioned the musical and opened it off Broadway. However ,it very quickly transferred to Broadway in September 2001.

The show was immensely successful, and was nominated in ten of the Drama Desk Awards in 2001. It was also nominated for no less than nine Tony Awards in 2002, winning three: Best Book of a Musical; Best Original Score;

?
is this really
the title?

URINETOWN
THE MUSICAL

[the original cast recording]

and Best Direction of a Musical for director John Rando. Actress Spencer Kayden also won the Theatre World Award for her performance in the show.

Urinetown is set in the fictional future, after a 20 year drought the government has enforced a ban on its cities private toilets in order to control water consumption. A corrupt private corporation called the Urine Good Company (UGC) enforces the public to use their pay-per-use amenities. Those who don't use the facilities are at high risk of being taken to Urinetown, no-one knows where this place is and no-one has ever returned.

When the fee increases to use one of the poorest and filthiest urinals in town, finally the oppressed masses rise up under the leadership of dashing young rebel Bobby Strong.

The production – which contains such show-stopping songs as "It's a Privilege to Pee" - had a limited well-received run at St James' Theatre in London from February to March 2014 under the guiding hand of director Jamie Lloyd.

West Side Story

Buoyed by Leonard Bernstein's score, and Stephen Sondheim's lyrics, West Side Story remains perhaps the most iconic of all the Shakespeare adaptations to visit the stage and big screen.

The musical West Side Story was written by American playwright Arthur Laurents in 1957, his inspiration coming from William Shakespeare's Romeo and Juliet.

The original concept to write a musical adaptation of Shakespeare's tragic romance came from Jerome Robbins who approached both Leonard Bernstein and Laurents to work together and create a musical adaptation.

Originally Robbins had proposed that the plot be focused on the conflict between an Irish Catholic family and that of a Jewish family living in the Lower East Side of Manhattan.

However on meeting with Bernstein at the Beverly Hills Hotel, he and Laurents decided to focus the musical on juvenile delinquent gangs after major coverage in the newspapers of the time covering stories of a Chicano turf war.

After Bernstein had decided solely to write the music, Stephen Sondheim was invited to write the lyrics and although he initially refused, it was Oscar Hammerstein who convinced him to accept.

Financing the production of West Side Story became increasingly difficult as many producers had turned it down. However, Stephen Sondheim convinced his friend and producer Hal Prince to fly to New York to hear the score and the rest, as they say, was history.

Bernstein also recalled that creatively,

the show was an impossible project: "We were told that no-one was going to able to sing augumented fourths as with 'Ma-ri-a'. Also, they said the score was too rangy for pop music ... Besides, who wanted to see a show in which the first-act curtain comes down on two dead bodies lying on the stage?... And then we had the really tough problem of casting it, because the characters had to be able not only to sing but dance and act and be taken for teenagers. Ultimately, some of the cast were teenagers, some were 21, some were 30 but looked 16. Some were wonderful singers but couldn't dance very well, or vice versa ... and if they could do both, they couldn't act."

The musical finally opened on Broadway in 1957 at the Winter Garden Theatre, directed and choreographed by Jerome Robbins and produced by Robert E Griffith and Hal Prince. The show was not initially critically acclaimed, with the creators' innovations in dance, music and theatrical style causing speculation as to how the production would influence the course of musical theatre. However the audiences were captivated and the production was nominated for six Tony Awards in 1958, winning two of them for Best Choreography and the Best Scenic

Design. It also won the Theatre World Award in the same year.

A film adaptation of the musical was released in 1961 receiving high praise from critics and the public alike. It was to become the second highest grossing film of the year in America, winning 10 Academy Awards from 11 nominations, including Best Picture. It still holds the title of the musical film with the most Academy Awards.

In London, West Side Story opened in 1958 at her Majesty's Theatre in The West End, directed and choreographed by Jerome Robbins and ran for a total of 1039 performances, closing in 1961.

The musical has been revived on many occasions and is currently touring the UK with a return to Liverpool planned for August 2014.

Wicked

The Wizard of Oz is considered to be one of the greatest musicals of all time. Showing that you can't get too much of a good thing, the spin-off musical Wicked has also been a box-office smash.

Wicked is based on the 1995 novel by Gregory Maguire called "Wicked: The Life and Times of the Wicked Witch of the West", a parallel novel to the original classic story, "The Wonderful Wizard of Oz", written by L Frank Baum in 1900.

Whilst reading Wicked on holiday, composer and lyricist Stephen Schwartz saw the potential to adapt the book into a musical and met with the author and asked him to release the rights to the book.

At the time, these were held by Universal Studios who had planned to make Wicked into a feature film. Schwartz convinced Universal's producers Marc Platt and David Stone to release the rights, with Platt becoming joint producer of the stage project.

The book follows two unlikely friends, the Wicked Witch of the East named Elphaba and the Good Witch of the North, named Glinda. The story is set in the land of Oz and is designed to ask the reader to think about what it is to be wicked.

Emmy award-winning writer Winnie Holzman was brought in by Schwartz and Platt to write a more succinct script from the novel's rather dense and complicated plot.

In 2003, after a pre-Broadway try-out at the Curran theatre in San Francisco, Wicked opened on Broadway at the Gershwin Theatre in October of the same year.

The show was hugely successful, winning 13 Tony Awards and six Drama Desk Awards with the cast album receiving a Grammy Award. In 2013, Wicked celebrated its 10th anniversary on Broadway, and is now the 11th of longest running Broadway show in history and has played for over 4155 performances.

The production of Wicked opened at the Apollo Victoria Theatre in London's West End in 2006. The show was due to finish in April 2014 and but would then go on a tour the UK.

The show has been a global phenomenum, winning 94 international awards. In London, it won the Olivier Award for the Most Popular Show and the Evening Standard Theatre Award for Best Night Out. In the Whatsonstage. com Awards ceremony, the show won eight awards, including Best West End Show and Best Musical.

Since its debut in 2003, Wicked has broken numerous box office records around the world, with the Broadway production earning $3.2 million by the end of its run in 2013.

The show has now been viewed in America and the UK by audiences of more than two million people.

Awards

Every year, the Laurence Olivier awards are presented by the Society of London Theatre. These awards were named after legendary British actor Laurence Olivier and are considered the highest honour in the British theatre - the equivalent of the Tony Awards, presented on New York's Broadway.

The Olivier awards were renamed as such in 1984 when Lord Olivier allowed his name to be used in place of the Society of West End theatre awards.

Most of the awards are judged by four panels, one each for theatre, opera, dance and 'affiliate'.

The judges for the theatre panel are chosen for their professional experience and specialist knowledge and are anonymous. However, each panel also includes eight members of the theatre-going public, four to judge plays and four to judge the musicals.

Within the opera, dance and affiliated panels must be three anonymous professional members to each judge their specialist area of expertise. Again, each panel must include two members of the theatre-going public.

Productions that wish to be eligible for the Laurence Olivier award nominations have to be produced in a theatre which is a member of the Society of London Theatre. The production must run for a minimum of 30 performances and premier between 16th February and 15th February of the following year. When a nomination has been received, it will have to be seconded by members of the society and only if successful, will be seen by the relevant judging panel.

A postal ballot of all members of the theatre panel and all members of the Society of London Theatre is used to decide nominations for the theatre categories. However for affiliate, opera and dance categories, nominations are to be decided in a secret ballot only by members of the relevant panel.

Within the musical category, there are six nominations for: Best New Musical, Best Musical Revival, Best Actor in a Musical, Best Actress in a Musical, Best Performance in a Supporting Role in a Musical and finally for the Outstanding Achievement in a Musical.

The award ceremony has been hosted by many famous venues, most commonly by the Grosvenor House Hotel which also houses the after show receptions, but presentations have also been held at the Victoria Palace, the Lyceum, the National Theatre, the Noel Coward, Shaftesbury, London Palladian, Dominion, Royalty, Theatre Royal Drury Lane, Cafe Royal, Piccadilly theatres and the Park Lane Hilton Hotel.

Famous presenters at the ceremony have included the likes of Michael Ball, Richard Wilson, Clive Anderson, Daniel Radcliffe, Anthony Hopkins, Sue Lawley, Diana Rigg and Angela Ripon.

There have been many notable records surrounding the Laurence Olivier awards. For example, the most Olivier awards ever to be received by a musical was Matilda, winning seven awards in 2012, including Best New Musical. In 2006, Billy Elliot received four Olivier awards, matching the 1999 performance of Oklahoma.

Few shows have been nominated 10 times, in fact Matilda and Hairspray being the only ones. Billy Elliot and Oklahoma were nominated nine times, with Guys and Dolls, My Fair Lady and Carousel all nominated eight times.

The special Olivier award for Lifetime Achievement was won by Andrew Lloyd Webber, who has also won six other Olivier awards.

Evening Standard Awards

The Evening Standard Theatre awards were sponsored by the Evening Standard newspapers in 1955 to annually present outstanding achievements in London's West End theatres.

The awards ceremonies are usually held in November and have been hosted by both the Savoy Hotel and the Royal Opera House.

In 2007 the award for Best Musical category was renamed the Ned Sherrin award, in memory of the famous broadcaster and raconteur who had for many years compered the Evening Standard awards' ceremonies.

Tony Awards

The Tony Award scheme is in actual fact the Antoinette Perry Award for Excellence in Theatre Awards, but more informally known as the Tony Awards, recognising achievement in Broadway theatre.

As with the Laurence Olivier awards, these are presented at the annual ceremony by the American Theatre Wing and the Broadway League. Antoinette Terry being the co-founder of the American Theatre Wing.

There are 26 categories of awards plus several special awards presented at the Tony Award ceremony, however initially only 11 awards were presented in 1947.

To be nominated or considered for a Tony Award is the highest theatre honour in the New York theatre industry and equivalent to the Academy Oscar awards in motion pictures.

Initially the award ceremony was held at the Waldorf Astoria hotel in New York City, 1947, but is now broadcast on American national television and has been held in various venues such as the Radio City Music Hall in New York City, then at the Gershwin Theatre and also the Beacon Theatre, more recently it has returned to the Radio City Music Hall for the last award ceremony in 2013.

The number and names of the various award categories have been changed many times over the years but there are now 26 categories and several special awards.

There are over 700 Tony Award voters, although these numbers vary slightly from year to year, the Tony Awards nominating committee can make nominations in various categories. The Tony Awards administration committee was set up to determine the eligibility for each nomination in the award categories, it has 24 members, 10 from the American Theatre Wing and 10 from the Broadway league with one each from the Dramatists Guild, Actors Equity Association, United Scenic Artists and the Society of Stage Directors and Choreographers.

The award ceremony is not without its controversies as several critics have suggested that the awards are purely a promotional vehicle for a few large production companies and theatre owners, only Broadway theatres that have 500 or more seats may be nominated for a Tony Award which limits the eligibility of many other productions.

Throughout the Tony Award history, only the musicals South Pacific and Hairspray have won all of the "big six" awards.

Most notable wins are for Hal Prince, who has won twenty one Tony Awards, eight for directing, eight for producing and two for being the Producer of the Year's Best Musical. He has also been awarded three special Tony Awards.

Drama Desk Awards

These awards were set up in 1955 to recognise the excellence of

any theatre production, unmindful of whether they were on or off Broadway.

Importantly, the Drama Desk Awards originate from a not for profit organisation and all the officers and nominating committee members perform their services on a voluntary basis.

**The pictures in this book were provided
courtesy of the following:**

WIKICOMMONS
commons.wikimedia.org

Design & Artwork by Scott Giarnese

Published by Demand Media Limited

Publishers: Jason Fenwick & Jules Gammond

Written by Janey Fletcher